HISTORY OF
PUBLIC SCHOOL MUSIC
IN
THE UNITED STATES

BY

EDWARD BAILEY BIRGE

Professor of Music, Indiana University

NEW AND AUGMENTED EDITION

MUSIC EDUCATORS NATIONAL CONFERENCE
1201 Sixteenth Street N.W., Washington, D.C. 20036

To M. T. B.

PREFACE

It is the purpose of this book to attempt to rescue from oblivion certain aspects of public school music which are fast becoming legendary. Available records of more than half of its history are few in number. Many of these exist only in the memories of people who were children in the middle periods of the nineteenth century. For these reasons the present volume endeavors to describe merely the main trend of the evolution of public school music, and to account as far as possible for the direction this evolution has taken.

The author wishes to acknowledge his indebtedness to colleagues and friends who have furnished him with valuable data and suggestions—among many others, to Peter W. Dykema for helpful criticisms of the first sketch of the book, to Osbourne McConathy, who in his youth was a friend and pupil of Luther Whiting Mason, for valuable information regarding his work and influence, and to Charles H. Farnsworth, for a copy of the Articles of Incorporation of the Musical Society of Thetford and Lime.

That this book may help to stimulate an interest in the historical background of music in the public schools is the earnest hope of the author.

Supplementing the above (the preface to the first edition of this book), the author wishes to acknowledge the help afforded more recently by several items of data in the manuscript volume *Lowell Mason—his Life and Work,* by Henry L. Mason, and in the brochure *The Educational Work of Dr. Lowell Mason,* by Theodore F. Seward.

Edward Bailey Birge

Bloomington, Indiana
January, 1937

CONTENTS

History of Public School Music in the United States

CHAPTER I

THE DEVELOPMENT OF THE SINGING-SCHOOL

DURING the four generations since 1838, when public school music was first introduced, nearly the whole of our educational history has been in the making. In that short space of ninety years we have fought four wars, have gone from stage-coach to flying-machine, from tallow dip to electric light, from the melodeon to the broadcasted concert of the radio, and from the district school with the three R's and a little singing for diversion, to a highly complex school system with music functioning in a dozen activities, and with high school orchestras playing symphonies and choruses singing the great oratorios. It will be worth our while to take a backward glance at an institution which at the beginning of this period was as universal as the crossroads country store and the village post-office, and which gave to school-music its first methods and all of its first teachers. This institution was the singing-school.

1

Public school music in the United States has its
roots in attempts to improve singing in the church
service. Though many of the early colonists must
have had musical gifts and appreciations, the cultivation of music among the early New Englanders and
in most of the other colonial settlements was not encouraged by the leaders of public opinion. Its
inherent power to give pleasure made it an object of
suspicion and well nigh prohibition for a long period.
For fully one hundred years after the first settlements there was no music education in the popular
sense of the term. Moreover, for many decades the
physical and social environment of the people prevented serious attention to music, even had there been
a desire for it; so that, as a matter of fact, here in
the wilderness of the "New World," separated from
the Mother country by three thousand miles of
ocean, musical culture throughout the seventeenth
century declined almost to the vanishing point.

The spiritual exaltation which sustained the
early settlers came through other channels than
music. Such music as they tolerated, was, to be
sure, of a strictly religious character, and was confined to congregational singing in the meeting-
houses, as the churches were called in New England.
There were no music-teachers, few if any instruments
of any kind, no singing societies, and little printed
music. The diversion of music and even less any
serious cultivation of the art, was no part of the life

of a people whose every-day business was that of subduing the forests, building homes, fighting the Indians, cultivating the soil, and providing for the bare necessities of life, matters which occupied all of their waking hours.

In Europe, during this period, music was undergoing a rapid development, but its cultivation was confined to the courts of kings and wealthy nobility, from which the people on this continent were far removed. We may well remember, too, as Mrs. Clark and other writers have pointed out, "that Jamestown and Plymouth Rock were contemporary with the very beginnings of modern music; that the first feeble attempts at opera and oratorio with a scant accompaniment of lutes, guitars, therabo, etc., were coincident with Jamestown, and were only just accomplished when the Pilgrims left England for Holland for their ten years' sojourn before coming to these bleak shores; if we can but remember that our century of colonization was the very same century that saw in Europe the work of Monteverde, Caccini, Scarlatti, Lully, Purcell and the rest, struggling for a new form of expression, new instruments, new combinations, new forms of writing music; if we can but remember that Haydn, who first grouped the instruments into families and developed the modern orchestra, was born the same year as our Washington who grouped the colonies into states—we may realize how very modern, after all, is music as we know it."[1]

Church music during the first colonial century consisted solely in the singing by the congregation of metrical versions of the Psalms. Only four or five tunes were in common use, such as *Old Hundred*, the *York Tune* and *Windsor*, and these were handed down by tradition. Hymns other than paraphrases of the Psalms were not known until after 1740, when Watts' and Wesley's hymns began to be reprinted in this country. Whether there was to be any singing at all was only settled after much controversy, and its enlightened defence by such ministers as Cotton, Mather, Symmes, Dwight and Eliot; for the clergy were the real leaders of opinion in all matters of common concern, religious, social, educational, and even political.

Until well into the eighteenth century singing in the church was in a crude and barbarous state. How bad it was we may gather from the words of one writer, who says, "Of all the dismal accompaniments of public worship in the early days of New England the music was the most hopelessly forlorn,—not only from the confused versifications of the Psalms which were used, but from the mournful monotony of the few known tunes and the horrible manner in which

[1]Frances E. Clark—*School Music*, 1836-1886-1911-1936—N. E. A. Proceedings for 1924.

these tunes were sung."[1]   Rev. Thomas Walter early in the eighteenth century writes, "The tunes are now miserably tortured and-twisted and quavered in our churches, into a horrid medley of confused and disorderly voices.   Our tunes are left to the mercy of every unskilled throat to chop and alter, to twist and change, according to their infinitely diverse and no less odd humours and fancies.   I have myself paused twice in one note to take a breath.   No two men in the congregation quaver alike or together.   It sounds in the ears of a good judge like five hundred tunes roared out at the same time, with perpetual interfearings with one another."[1]   To such chaos had isolation from the centers of musical culture brought the divine art.

The fact, however, that the second book printed in America was *The Bay Psalm Book*, a metrical version of the Psalms, prepared by Revs. John Eliot, Thomas Weld, and Richard Mather, and published in 1640, shows that music was not wholly without significance in the seventeenth century. This book was without music, however, until the ninth edition, printed in 1698, which contained thirteen tunes in two-part harmony. "This crudely printed book, without bars except at the end of each line, is the oldest existing music of American imprint."[2]

[1]Alice Morse Earle — *The Sabbath in Puritan New England* — Scribners, 1896.
[2]William Arms Fisher—*Notes on Music in Old Boston*—Oliver Ditson Company, 1918.

Congregational singing was conducted by "lining out the tune." It became the established custom in all New England churches for some leader to read the words of the psalm one line at a time, followed by the people. The custom originated in England for the benefit of those who could not read. Crude as it was, this device at least enabled the singers to begin each phrase together. The musical result, as has already been noted, was barbarously crude.

Toward the close of the seventeenth century a desire for improvement began to be felt in many quarters. Influenced doubtless by the appearance in 1698 of the new edition of *The Bay Psalm Book* containing music, a spirited agitation began for singing by "rule and art," and the "recall of notes," as music reading was then termed. We are told, however, that the attempts to thus improve musical performance "met with violent opposition. Many congregations were almost split on the question. The storm spent its greatest fury in Massachusetts, dividing congregations and arraying ministers and people, deacons and choirs in the utmost hostility against each other."[1]

The reformers finally won their point, and we learn that as early as 1723, "the churches of Boston, Roxbury, Dorchester, Cambridge, Taunton, Bridge-

[1] N. H. Allen—*Old Time Music and Musicians*—Connecticut Quarterly, 1895.

water, Charlestown, Ipswich, Newbury, Andover, Bradford and some other places, had commenced singing by "rule and art."[1] From this advance in musical standards other improvements gradually followed.. The better singers began to sit together in a group; out of this grew the idea of a choir, and finally the choir was given formal recognition and seated in a gallery. The betterment of congregational singing under the leadership of the choir rendered unnecessary continuing the "lining out" practice, though the custom died hard and only after a bitter controversy.

Out of this condition of affairs and the urgent need of instruction in the rudiments of music emerged the singing-school. The first practical instruction book on singing was written by Rev. John Tufts, of Newbury, and issued in Boston about 1712. It was entitled "*A very plain and easy Introduction to the Art of Singing Psalm Tunes; With the Cantus, or Trebles, of Twenty-eight Psalm Tunes contrived in such a manner as that the Learner may attain the Skill of Singing them with the greatest ease and Speed imaginable.* Price, 6d, or 5s, the dozen."[2] It was very successful and was reprinted in many editions, though it used a letter notation, M, F, S, L, (for mi, fa, sol, la) on the staff instead of

---

[1]*Boston Musical Gazette,* February 6, 1839.

[2]William Arms Fisher—*Notes on Music in Old Boston*—Oliver Ditson Company, 1918.

notes, thus anticipating the Tonic Sol-fa notation by more than a hundred years.   The first instruction book with printed music, said to be the first music printed with bar-lines in America, was by Rev. Thomas Walter of Roxbury, and was entitled *The Grounds and Rules of Musick explained, or an Introduction to the art of singing by note.*   It was published in 1721 from the press of J. Franklin, brother of Benjamin, then a lad of fifteen.[1]

One of the most persistent advocates of the singing-school was the Rev. Thomas Symmes, who with tongue and pen urged their establishment.   In an essay published in 1723 his plea takes the form of the following questions—"Would it not greatly tend to promote singing of psalms if singing-schools were promoted?   Would not this be conforming to scripture pattern?   Have we not as much need of them as God's people of old?   Have we any reason to expect to be inspired with the gift of singing, any more than that of reading?"[2]   Through such advocacy of singing-schools as a means of improving music in public worship they began to be established about 1720.   In that year Handel and Bach had each attained the age of thirty-five and were composing their immortal masterpieces.   It was not until eleven

[1]William Arms Fisher — *Notes on Music in Old Boston* — Oliver Ditson Company, 1918.

[2]*The Art of Music, Vol. IV*—Daniel Gregory Mason—Music in America, page 26.

years later, that the first recorded concert was given in America. This was in Boston, in December, 1731.[1]

Exact data regarding the formation of singing-schools are scanty and meager. But with the growing sentiment in favor of singing by "rule and art," it is probable that they were started in the churches which successively introduced the new kind of singing. Such records as are available show that John Salter was teaching a singing class in Charleston, S. C., in 1730, that William Tuckey held singing classes in New York in 1754, that Josiah Davenport was teaching singing in Philadelphia in 1757, and that the more celebrated James Lyon began his work in the same city in 1750, and that the Moravians started singing-schools at Bethlehem, Pa., as early as 1750. "From the diaries of Franklin, Washington, Samuel Adams and other prominent men of the colonial period, much may be learned of the powerful impression which the music of the Bethlemites made upon those who came into contact with it."[2]

"In 1764 the children of Philadelphia were receiving instruction in the art of psalmody, for the vestry board of St. Peter's and Christ Church extended a vote of thanks to Francis Hopkinson and to

[1]Henry C. Lahee—*Annals of Music in America*—Marshall Jones Company, 1922.
[2]*American History and Encyclopedia of Music*—History of American Music.

William Young for their kind services in teaching and instructing the children in psalmody."[1]   Other items of record are that Hugh Maguire had singing classes at St. Anne's Church in Baltimore in 1765, that a school master named Bradford had a singing-school at Newport, R. I., in 1770, and Samuel Wadsworth one at Salem in 1772.   In 1784 Andrew Adgate established a singing-school at Philadelphia which was entitled "An Institution for the Encouragement of Church Music."   It soon ceased to exist; but Adgate immediately organized free classes which flourished for many years.   The enthusiasm of Andrew Adgate, Francis Hopkinson, and James Lyon left an influence which was felt for more than fifty years.[1]   We know also that William Billings, the second American Composer, (Francis Hopkinson being the first) organized a singing-school at Stoughton, Mass., which grew into the Stoughton Musical Society in 1786.   This society is still flourishing, probably the oldest musical organization in America having a continuous existence.   In 1790 the Dorchester society challenged the Stoughton society to a contest, in which Stoughton won by singing the *Hallelujah Chorus* from memory.

Such are some of the fragmentary data regarding the establishment of the singing-school movement in America.   They cover a period of sixty years,

[1]*American History and Encyclopedia of Music*—History of American Music.

during which the colonial wars had been fought, the Revolutionary War had wrested independence from the Mother country, and the Constitution had been made and adopted. The scattered colonies had become a nation.

Meanwhile the singing-school had justified its existence and had become a popular institution. Starting in Boston, it had spread through New England and the other colonies. It began as a crude choir school. But though the religious influence was paramount for a long period, it progressively adapted itself to the currents of social and political feeling which from one generation to another affected the common life of the people. It was truly educational in that both of its major aims, the study of choral music and acquiring the art of music reading, laid the national foundations for musical culture and appreciation, the full strength of which did not become evident until the next period. And when we reflect that until music began to be taught in the public schools, the singing-school was the sole means of musical instruction in the popular sense of the word, that from the beginning it was allied with the church, the center of the social as well as the religious life of the community and that old and young were drawn to it for the pleasure of singing together and for social intercourse, some of the reasons for its growth and its tenacious hold upon the affections of the people become plain.

Though it grew to be a truly national institution, the singing-school remained from first to last a private enterprise. The teacher organized his own classes, which were generally held at night, taught them, and collected his modest fees. During the day time he worked at some other occupation. In fact, during the entire first century of its existence, singing-school teaching was more of an avocation than a profession, perhaps because of the fact that the profession of musician was not generally regarded with favor. William Billings was a tanner by trade, Oliver Holden was a carpenter; Daniel Reid was a comb maker, and Jacob Kimball a lawyer. Later, toward the middle of the nineteenth century the general attitude regarding music as a profession underwent a marked change toward tolerance and even approval.

Historians give only an occasional glimpse of the actual conducting of a singing-school. Moses Cheney, born in 1776, and later very active as a singing-school teacher, describes in a letter the starting of one which he attended. "The sessions were held either in the homes of the members or in the school house. At the first meeting boards were placed on kitchen chairs to answer for seats and all the candidates for membership paraded around the room in a circle, the singing master in the center. The master then read the rules, instructing all to pay attention to the rising and falling of the notes.

Books containing individual parts, treble, counter, tenor and bass were distributed, and directions for pitch were given. Then the master commenced. 'Now follow me right up and down; sound.' So the master sounded and the pupils sounded and in this way some learned to sing by note and others by imitation. At the close of the session the singing master agreed to give instruction for one shilling and six pence per night and to take his pay in Indian corn."[1]

Advertisements from newspapers early in the nineteenth century show something of the method of getting a class together. The following are from the *Cincinnati Western Spy*: — "Those gentlemen and ladies who feel themselves disposed to organize a singing-school will please to convene at the court house tomorrow evening at candle light, as it is proposed to have a singing. Those who have books will please bring them." A Mr. MacLean's advertisement states that all persons desiring to join his class "may become members at the honorarium of one dollar each for thirteen nights, or two dollars per quarter," and that "subscribers are to find their own wood and coal."

The following gem is from a middle western paper of the early eighteen fifties:—"All those who wish to be taught music in classes as it was taught in ancient times by Haydn, Handel, Mozart, Beethoven

[1] *American History and Encyclopedia of Music*—Music in America.

and Mendelssohn, and as it is taught in modern times by Mason, Webb, Hastings, Bradbury and Zeuner, will gather this evening for the first meeting."[1]

The change in church singing from "lining out the tune" to singing by the "recall of notes" led to the formation not only of singing-schools but also of singing societies, and probably at first more frequently the latter, on account of a lack of teachers. And very often a singing-school would change into a singing society, as was the case with the Stoughton singing-school, and vice versa. The only difference between the two kinds of groups was that the singing-school gave intensive study to music reading in addition to practice in singing. Both used the same music material, namely, psalm tunes.

The character of the aims of the early singing societies is shown in the following introduction to the articles of organization of the Musical Society in Thetford and Lime, which dates from 1781; — "Whereas God has clearly made it known in the established laws of Nature & in his holy word to be his mind and will that his rational creatures Should praise him with vocal musick & thereby made it our duty to learn those rules which are necessary to regulate us in the Skillfull & right performance of this part of divine worship And considering that the End & Design of Musick is to quicken, enliven & animate our Devotion in Worshiping God & has a

most powerful tendency to raise our cold affection to
a divine Ardour & also that Musick has a tendency
to promote many other valuable Ends & purposes, &
further Considering our great backwardness to the
right performance of this important Duty, we have
thought proper to draw up the following Articles
with a view hereby to Cultivate, keep up & bring to
perfection more especially the practical part of
Musick and therefore we whose names are underwrit-
ten do view & declare ourselves as firmly bound to
observe the following articles as our own promises
and Honor can bind us."

The aims of the singing-school controlled the
make up and contents of the tune books, as the instruction books were called.   These consisted of a
section devoted to an exposition of the elements of
notation with exercises for practice, and a miscel-
laneous selection of psalm tunes and anthems.   In
due time glees and part songs began to be included,
and the section devoted to the rudiments underwent
a continuous development in the way of logical presentation of the subject.

The first tune books of which we have record
began to appear about 1760.   Between that date
and 1780 about fourteen were published, more than
sixty between 1780 and 1800 and about one hundred
in the first ten years of the nineteenth century.
These figures show in no uncertain terms the growing
vogue of the singing-school.   At the height of its

popularity and influence the output of tune books was enormous. The *American Supplement of Grove's Dictionary of Music and Musicians* lists the titles of some 375 of these books by about 200 known compilers. Most of the compilers were themselves singing-school teachers, prominent among whom in the early history of the movement were James Lyon, of Philadelphia, whose *Urania* dates from 1762, and William Billings, of Boston, who produced his *New England Psalm Singer* in 1770, *The Singing Master's Assistant* in 1776, and several other books, all containing much original music of his own. Similar books by Andrew Law, Daniel Reid, Timothy Swan, Andrew Adgate, Samuel A. Holyoke, and Oliver Holden appeared near the end of the eighteenth century. Oliver Holden's tune *Coronation* still holds its place in our modern hymn books.

The style of psalm tune most cultivated by the native composers of the last decades of the eighteenth century was the so-called "fuguing tune," of which hundreds were written and which were very popular at the time. This style of music comprised almost the entire repertory of the church choirs of the period. The "fuguing tunes" tickled the vanity of the singers by affording an opportunity for vocal display which was little edifying to the spirit of worship.

The musical theory incorporated into the early tune books by Billings and his contemporaries was taken exclusively from similar books written by Playford, Tansur, Williams and other English music teachers and editors. The singing syllables used were mi-fa-sol-la, which in England had supplanted the older hexachord system consisting of the six syllables ut-re-mi-fa-sol-la. The mi-fa-sol-la method was cumbersome and confusing, because it did not use a different syllable for each tone of the scale. The first attempt to introduce the continental system of the seven scale syllables do-re-mi-fa-sol-la-si was made in *The Massachusetts Compiler*, published in 1796 and edited by Oliver Holden, Samuel Holyoke and Hans Gram. This book was influential in displacing the mi-fa-sol-la system and thus making possible a musical theory which all could understand. The seven syllable system was introduced in England early in the nineteenth century and was used by John Hullah in his singing classes and beginning in 1840 was incorporated in the still more popular Tonic Sol-fa method of John Curwen.

Most of the early singing teachers, like William Billings, were self taught, for opportunities for instruction were scanty. But though their musical knowledge and culture were not of European standard, it was sufficient to make them effective leaders, reinforced as it was by personal initiative and interest in musical progress. They taught the people the rudiments of music, each in his own way, and in his own field. Collectively they did a useful and indespensable work; for they not only helped to bring order out of chaos in church singing, but they laid the first foundations of technical knowledge of music, they kindled the musical imagination of the people, and afforded glimpses of some of the artistic possibilities latent within themselves.   This group of singing teachers belonged to the period just following the American Revolution.   They were the forerunners of another and better trained group, whose attitude, method and influence were largely inspired by Lowell Mason.

Of the contemporaries of Lowell Mason who were independently influential in this movement the two most prominent were Thomas Hastings and Nathaniel N. Gould, Hastings in New York State and Gould in Massachusetts and New Hampshire. Both were famous and popular teachers, composers and compilers of many collections of tune books. Gould was the author of a *History of Church Music in America,* and was one of the first to organize juvenile choirs.

Lowell Mason was born in Medfield, Massachusetts, January 8, 1792, three years after the national constitution had been ratified and Washington had taken the oath of office as first president, a stirring time in which to be born.   He early showed evidence of unusual musical gifts, and began teaching singing while a mere youth.   In 1812, when he was twenty years of age, he was sent to Savannah, Georgia,

where he was employed in a bank.   Here he remained
fifteen years, devoting all his leisure time in teaching
singing classes, composing music and leading church
choirs.   He gathered the material for a new church
music book and took it to Boston, where it was published as *The Handel and Haydn Collection* with the
co-operation of the Handel and Haydn Society.
This collection marked a new epoch in church music.
It had an extraordinarily wide sale, bringing the
author immediately into prominence as a choral authority, and was probably the decisive factor in deciding his future career.   At any rate he became a
marked man, and his success as a choir leader in
Savannah led to his being called to Boston in 1827
to have charge of the music in three churches, of
which one was Dr. Lyman Beecher's.   Here, at
thirty-seven years of age, he became for twenty-five
years the central figure of a period of musical progress which was unique because of its national scope.

The times were ripe for a musical advance.
The singing-school had demonstrated its value as a
means of popular education; the Handel and Haydn
Society had begun its work in 1815, and was making
popular the oratorios of these great composers; Boston had heard the Haydn symphonies under the
leadership of Gottlieb Graupner, a sterling musician
who had been oboist in Haydn's London orchestra,
and who had settled in Boston in 1800.   Public concerts were becoming numerous in all the larger cities,

and opera had been heard in New York and other centers. European musicians were beginning to come over to stay as teachers and performers.

Of equal significance was the fact that with the opening up of the national domain beyond the Alleghanies, streams of immigration from New England and the other states had poured into western New York and the Ohio valley, and were rapidly creating new commonwealths as far west as the Mississippi. The settlers of these new lands carried with them their cherished institutions—the town meeting, the school, the church, and the singing-school.

The period of musical progress upon which Lowell Mason was entering as the leading spirit developed the singing-school to the height of its vogue and influence. It was the period of the itinerant singing-school teacher, who carried on his work in the winter evenings, with a circuit of several towns. Teaching singing-school became a real profession during this period. This was the singing-school which our grandparents knew, and which is thus described by Henry S. Perkins,—"It is interesting to retrospect our early singing-school experience, when old and young, great and small, piled into a big box upon the bob-sled with a generous quantity of straw upon the bottom and buffalo robes over us with many other wraps to shield us from the twenty degrees of coolness, and the sled being hauled by a yoke of well-bred oxen down the steep hill two miles to the valley school house by the side of a stony brook where the interested class assembled once a week through the long winter. We not only sang every exercise, tune and anthem, to do, re, mi, with a tallow candle firmly standing upon the back of the desk to furnish us with what John G. Saxe, the Vermont poet, called 'The Light of Other Days,' but at the close, after father had invoked the divine blessing upon the school and the efforts which had been made to cultivate the heart and hand, we escorted the prettiest girl, to our thinking, home, especially if she was going our way, and we got ahead of the other fellows below. We could only stop at the door long enough to say one 'good night,' for we must catch up with the ox team."

"Those were halycon days. We learned to read and sing from the musical notation at first sight. My father was a methodical man, a thorough disciplinarian, a 'Major General, Commanding,' and unwaveringly pious, yet he allowed us to fiddle anything from the *Irish Washerwoman* to the *Devil's Dream*, except on Sunday."[1]

Another somewhat similar picture of the singing-school of pre-Civil War days is given by W. J. Baltzell. "It was the custom to have a singing-school every winter in different communities, and this naturally formed a gathering point for the young people from villages and farms covering a consider-

[1] *School Music*—May, 1908.

able radius.   Snow on the ground, a sleigh, and a
fine horse, made a combination which brought the
young people out to any gathering where there
might be some social diversion.   Therefore the singing-school was really a focal point for the recrea-
tional activities of the community.   Of course the
membership was not confined to the youth of the
comm inity.   On the contrary, one would find in the
class persons of various ages from boys and girls of
nine and ten up to grandfathers and grandmothers."

"The instruction consisted of some elementary
rules for singing and for the rudiments of music as
relating to reading from note, according to the Sol-fa
syllables.   The singers were taught to beat time for
themselves and to follow their own voice parts.   They
were usually much in earnest, the majority of them
learning to read music with some degree of skill.   Of
the quality of their singing perhaps one should not
say much.   Quantity was more generally the rule
than quality."

"Many persons of the present day are inclined
to smile at the work done in these old time singing-
schools.   It is fair to say that for their advantages
they did really good work.   The members were
limited in their knowledge of music and their ability
to read difficult music, but for their own purpose—
that of singing the church and Sunday School music
of the time—they were well equipped.   We must not
forget that the singing-school represents a movement

to take to the people music in a simple, practical form, in which they could take part acceptably—which is the essential in all popular music education."[1]

The following extract is from page 160 of Ritter's *Music in America*. "That peculiar American trait of trying to reduce everything that seems complicated, and takes, as such, considerable time to master, to a great simplicity of system, in order to learn it quickly, and save time, has also induced many of the psalm-tune teachers to endeavor to devise simple and short methods for the study of the rudimenta of music. One does away with the lines of the staff; one changes the position of the clefs; another invents new forms of musical characters—patent notes; now the flats, now the sharps are found too embarassing to the impatient learner, and are done away with; the whole staff, notes and all, are swept away, and replaced by figures; a teacher becomes aware of the fact that the tenor never finds his place in the four-part setting of a hymn-tune; a new form of clef is invented to obviate that difficulty, etc. And of course we are told, that, by means of such new and 'indispensable methods,' the study of music will be found to be merely child's play; but after a little while the new system fails to meet the 'much-felt want,' and is after a little trial again quietly put

[1] W. J. Baltzell—*Old Time Community Music*—M. T. N. A. Proceedings, 1922.

away. It does not prove a successful speculation;
and a sensible return to the 'old-fashioned' method is
generally the result of all such attempts."

The patent notes referred to in the above extract, and sometimes called shaped notes or buck-
wheat notes, had considerable notational vogue at one
period and are still in use in some mountain regions

1. All hail the pow'r of Je - sus' name! Let an - gels pros-trate fall;
2. Let ev - 'ry kin-dred, ev - 'ry tribe, On this ter - res- trial ball;
3. O that with yon - der sa-cred throng We at His feet may fall!

Bring forth the roy - al di - a - dem, And crown Him Lord of   all,
To   Him all maj - es - ty as-cribe, And crown Him Lord of   all,
We'll join the ev - er - last-ing song, And crown Him Lord of   all,

Bring forth the roy-al di - a - dem, And crown Him Lord of all.
To   Him all maj-es - ty as-cribe, And crown Him Lord   of all.
We'll join the ev - er - last-ing song, And crown Him Lord   of all.

Coronation, printed in shaped notes.

of the Southern states. This notation, which seems to have been invented by Andrew Law, a contemporary of William Billings, used a different shaped note head for each tone of the scale. It is one of the curiosities of notational history.

When Mr. Mason came to Boston, he immediately set out to do two things, to raise the standard of singing-school teaching, which he regarded as the foundation of popular music education, and to improve the quality of church music material and of choir singing. He himself, in addition to his choir work, held large singing classes, in which he demonstrated his methods of teaching. There quickly gathered about him an ardent group of admiring pupils, themselves many of them singing-school teachers, of whom several became his assistants.

Public minded citizens of Boston became impressed with the vital importance of Mr. Mason's work, which had grown to include children's classes, and a group of them, headed by Samuel A. Eliot, mayor of Boston, and father of Harvard's famous president, founded the Boston Academy of Music in the latter part of the year 1832, for the purpose of giving the work greater scope and influence. This was the first school of music pedagogy in the United States. In the short space of fourteen years, it accomplished work of paramount importance, and then ceased to exist. It was founded for certain definite purposes, and when these were realized, its work

passed on to other channels.   These purposes were
as follows,—to teach the art of singing, to teach the
rudiments of thorough bass and harmony, to expound
the methods of teaching singing-schools and conducting choral music, and to promote the introduction
of music in the public schools.   This last achievement,
the crowning work of the Academy, will be the theme
of the next chapter of this book.   The Academy
trained choruses of adults and of children and maintained an orchestra, which had the distinction of
giving Boston its first performance of a Beethoven
symphony.

Meanwhile, for several years beginning in 1829
groups of singing-schools and societies met in
Concord, N. H., and other centers, under the leadership of Henry E. Moore, and held what they called
a Singing-School Convention.   This was the beginning of the convention movement, which later spread
so rapidly to all parts of the country.   Even from
the beginning these gatherings called attention to
some hitherto unrealized possibilities in the singing
teaching profession, such as the value of group discussion, the potency of the magnetic platform lecturer and teacher, and the inspiration of large group
singing under an inspiring leader.

Lowell Mason quickly realized the values inherent in the convention idea, and with his instinct
for leadership proceeded to make the Academy of

Music the center of the new movement.   In 1834 he issued his famous *Manual of Instruction*, which

CHAPTER VIII.

EXERCISES ON THE THIRD.

§ 223. The scale occupies a similar place in mnsic, to that which the alphabet does in written language. As in reading, we are able immediately to give the proper sound to each letter ; so in singing, we must also acquire such a readiness, that we can, at once, give the proper sound to each note we see in connexion with others on the staff.

§ 224. Sing the first three notes of the scale with the syllables *do, re, mi*. Sing three and repeat it twice.

Sing, 1 3, 1 3 1, 3 1 3, 1 1 3 3, 3 3 1 1.

I will now write these sounds one and three on the staff.

On what line or space does 3 stand ?

By what letter is it designated ?

§ 225. The teacher now writes on the staff the following exercises, and requires them to be sung : first, perhaps by small divisions of scholars, or by individuals, either voluntarily or by request, afterwards by all in chorus : at one time with the appropriate syllables, at another with *la*, at another with numerals, and again with letters.

Page from Mason's *Manual of the Boston Academy of Music,* 1834.

became the handbook of every singing-school teacher, and in 1836 he organized a convention at the Academy, making use of discussions and lectures.

To the annual conventions of the Academy were attracted hundreds of teachers from far and near, and
here was gradually elaborated a form of program
which became the typical convention type of procedure for many decades.   This was a session of
about four days, with three sessions each day.
These were used for lectures on methods of teaching,
open discussion of problems, classes in the study of
psalmody, of harmony, and of voice culture.   The
evening sessions were usually devoted to choral practice which culminated in a concert at the end of the
convention.   In 1840 the Academy convention was
organized under the name of "The National Music
Convention."   From this time on conventions began
to multiply in the same way as had the singing-schools
out of which they developed.   They offered a new
and alluring field of activity to men who had strength
of leadership and power to sway an audience, and it
is no exaggeration to say that most of the men who
displayed such powers and became noted convention
leaders were trained or directly influenced by Lowell
Mason.

Just as the singing-school gave the nation its
first school in the rudiments of music, so the Music
Convention became our first national school of music
pedagogy, harmony, conducting and voice culture,
and thousands of young people in all parts of the
country received training in these fundamentals
under the leadership of such men as Thomas

Hastings, George J. Webb, William B. Bradbury, George F. Root, Isaac B. Woodbury, Benjamin F. Baker and Luther O. Emerson, all of whom possessed outstanding qualities of leadership. They were all authors of many tune books and collections, for which there was a continuous demand; most of them were composers of merit, and Webb, Bradbury, and Root had some years of study with European teachers.

In his editorship of collections for singing-schools and the church, and his original compositions in the field of hymnology, Lowell Mason set a standard which places him apart from all his contemporaries, and gives him an enduring position as an American composer. Many of our best beloved hymns are from his pen. His style was deliberately simple, and hence, effective and enduring. He found time in his busy life as teacher and lecturer to write hundreds of sacred and secular compositions, to publish over thirty books of music, and to travel extensively in Europe.

The great vogue of the Musical Convention covered a period of about thirty years beginning in the forties. Its influence was felt in every section as far west as the Mississippi and as far south as Virginia. Wherever a convention was held, it tended to quicken the musical life of the community and to make it a center of influence. Regarding this influence C. M. Cady, of Chicago, writing to his friend H.

S. Perkins said, "For 30 years I have watched the effects of these gatherings upon cities, counties and states in which they have been held under such men as Hastings, Mason, Woodbury, Root and a host of younger conductors. Without exception, so far as my observation has extended, they have resulted in good in many ways, prominent among which are the following:—

1.   They have inspired participants with enthusiasm for musical improvement, whether as individuals, choirs, or congregations, and buried petty jealousies under lofty aims.

2.   They have not only led to better voice culture, better choirs and heartier congregational singing, but have been powerful agents in the introduction of sight singing into the public schools.

3.   They have familiarized the public with grand choral effects and the works of the great masters, and to that extent shown the superiority of the sublime over the merely pretty and beautiful."[1]

The convention movement was not without its extravagances and absurdities. Being an institution of, by and for the people, and without control or supervision, it was subject to wide variations in educational merit, from the highly organized convention of Mason and Root, to the feeblest of

[1]H. S. Perkin's address at M. T. N. A. in 1887.

imitations. The early exigencies of the singing-school tended of necessity to make every singing-school teacher a song book compiler. But this tendency persisted long after the necessity had ceased. The superior collections of Mason, Bradbury and Root were imitated by scores of inferior collections. In many cases conventions seem to have been held more for the purpose of exploiting the sale of a new singing book than for any clearly musical purpose.

Though organized to give instruction along several lines, a study of the convention development shows that it appealed to two main types of interest, namely, pedagogical and choral, and that its adherents and students were drawn to it more or less from one or the other of these motives. It soon developed that in many instances those who came for pedagogy wanted more teaching and less choral practice, while those who came for choral practice wanted more singing and less pedagogy. This situation led, especially under the leadership of Mason and Root, to another type of convention, the normal institute, whose sessions ran for several weeks. Mr. Mason held a normal institute in New York City in 1851 which lasted for three months, and drew students from all over the United States. The normal institutes were purely pedagogical enterprises, and like the conventions, soon became numerous and popular. They offered courses in methods, theory, voice and piano, much like the year-round conservatory, into which many of them later developed. The fact that such musicians as William Mason, William H. Sherwood, Frederick W. Root, W. S. B. Mathews, and Julia Ettie Crane were on their teaching staff indicates the standard of work they offered. The institutes were usually held during the summer, and there was a tendency for the terms convention and musical institute to be used interchangeably.

Just as the pedagogical side of the convention grew into pedagogical institutions, the choral side tended to develop into choral organizations. One of the best examples of this is the Worcester Festival, which has undergone a complete development from a singing-school convention into a choral festival. It started in 1858 as the Worcester Musical Convention, under the leadership of Benjamin F. Baker of Boston, and Edward Hamilton of Worcester. In course of time the choral activities became more and more important, until in 1866 Carl Zerrahn became choral conductor, while one or two singing-school teachers continued to take care of the instruction side of the work. Finally about a decade later, the singing-school features disappeared entirely, and it became the three days' choral festival which it has remained ever since.

It would be difficult to exaggerate the importance of the musical convention during the period from twenty-five years before the Civil War to a decade thereafter.   During this period the movement reached every section of the country, training singing-school teachers, agitating the introduction of music into the public schools, giving instruction in harmony, in the art of singing, and in its later form of Normal Institute it became a short term conservatory of music.   Above all, the convention made the people realize the nobility of the great oratorios and planted the seed of serious choral work.   "The music studied in these conventions included choruses from the oratorios such as *Samson, Messiah, Israel in Egypt, Hymn of Praise, Forty-Second Psalm, Elijah, Hear My Prayer, Creation,* Rossini's *Stabat Mater,* English Glees, and opera choruses.   A program made of this quality of music speaks well for the musicianship of the directors, their general scholarship, and especially for the devotion of the singers."[1]

The singing-school and its child, the musical convention, have disappeared.   They exist only as a tradition.   But though they have gone, their spirit goes on in the institutions which supplanted them, public school music, the summer music school, the musical conservatory, the great music teachers' associations, and many choral societies.   They were peculiarly American institutions.

The singing-school especially, together with the

[1]W. J. Baltzell—*Old Time Community Music*—M. T. N. A. Proceedings, 1922.

music written for its use by generations of American psalmodists, came into being in response to instinctive cravings for a folk expression on this continent, corresponding to that which has produced the musical culture and folk music of Europe. Beginning with a crude attempt to improve congregational singing, it produced, during one hundred and fifty years of progressive development, results creditable to American music education. It gradually developed a highly skillful teaching technique, entirely adequate to prepare, in twenty lessons, a creditable concert program, besides a review of the rudiments of music, and a successful initiation into the mysteries of music reading. Many people, and sometimes whole families, attended the singing-school year after year, which accounts for the fact that in each community there were a considerable number who were familiar with some oratorio music and who were good music readers. It also explains the fact that many singing societies developed directly from the singing-school. As a popular means of instruction, the nature of its mission removed the singing-school from the fields of high musical achievement possible only through intensive and long continued effort, but it undoubtedly laid the foundations upon which such attainment rests.

CHAPTER II

THE MAGNA CHARTA OF MUSIC
EDUCATION IN AMERICA

MUSIC was the first of the expressive subjects
to take its place in the curriculum of the public schools. The fact that this could occur at a time
when the value of a school subject in practical every-
day affairs was the criterion by which it was judged
is evidence that music had become so strongly inter-
woven in community life that its utility could be
taken for granted. Indeed, it is noticeable that the
advocates of the introduction of music into the schools
always built up their arguments on a basis of practical rather than aesthetic values, though they did not
wholly ignore the latter.

Beyond the memory of the oldest inhabitant the
singing-school had been teaching the elements of
music; and there was evidence on every hand of its
effectiveness. But though it was a popular institution, only a small and selective minority of the people
actually attended the singing-school. It became
something like the elective music class of our modern
high school, and there had come about a well indoc-

trinated belief that only a talented few possessed a musical ear, and this fact conferred a pleasurable sense of distinction on those who could sing and read

LOWELL MASON

music.   It was the mission of Lowell Mason to break down the doctrine of the talented few, and to show that its foundations were largely mythical.

It must not be supposed that the idea of public school music belonged exclusively to one man or group of men, either in Boston or any where else. On the contrary, the fact that it was being thought about as a desirable study in many quarters is shown by the comparative rapidity with which its introduction took place, after the agitation for it took organized form. In Boston, public opinion as represented by leading citizens, was ready to approve giving the introduction of music a trial. All that was necessary was a successful demonstration and firm leadership. The demonstration was furnished by Lowell Mason. The leadership which kept the issue before the public came both from him and his associate directors of the Academy of Music.

Agitation of the question was started in 1830, by William C. Woodbridge, by an address delivered in Boston, on *Vocal Music as a Branch of Common Education*, illustrations being given by children trained by Lowell Mason. Mr. Woodbridge had recently spent some time in Europe in studying methods of instruction in the schools. He had visited Switzerland, where he had seen the work of Johann George Nageli, who was applying the principles of Pestalozzi to the teaching of music. His own favorable opinion, confirmed by that of educational leaders in Switzerland and Germany, convinced him that music ought to have a place in the American school curriculum. He attempted to start the work in Hartford in 1830 with Elam Ives as teacher, but with what result no records are available. But he soon placed the carrying out of his ideas in the hands of Lowell Mason, whose skill in teaching children and whose standing as a musician made him the logical leader in the enterprise. Mr. Mason became convinced of the soundness of the Pestalozzian principles, and their practicability in teaching singing, and incorporated them in his *Manual of Instruction*. The principles thus formulated are the following:—

1.   To teach sounds before signs—to make the child sing before he learns the written notes or their names.

2.   To lead him to observe, by hearing and imitating sounds, their resemblances and differences, their agreeable and disagreeable effect, instead of explaining these things to him—in short, to make him active instead of passive in learning.

3.   To teach but one thing at a time—rhythm, melody, expression being taught and practiced separately before the child is called to the difficult task of attending to all at once.

4.   To make them practice each step of each of these divisions, until they are master of it, before passing to the next.

5.   To give the principles and theory after practice, and as an induction from it.

6.   To analyze and practice the elements of articulate sound in order to apply them to music.

7.   To have the names of the notes correspond to those used in instrumental music.[1]

This was the first formulation of modern principles of teaching music in the United States (1834).

About the year 1832 Lowell Mason's "Juvenile Choir" began to sing in public concerts, creating, as we are told a prodigious sensation and exploding unceremoniously the old idea of "only here and there a musical ear."[2]   Everything now seemed favorable for pushing to a conclusion the matter of introducing music in the schools, and "Mr. George H. Snelling, in behalf of a special committee appointed for that purpose, presented to the Primary School Board of Boston an elaborate report strongly urging the adoption of music as a regular study in the primary schools."[2]   The following resolution was submitted,— "Resolved that one school from each district be selected for the introduction of systematic instruction in vocal music under the direction of a committee to consist of one from each district and two from the standing committee."[3]   Apparently no formal action was taken on the resolution, and the matter was dropped, though some experimental lessons in music were given in the schools.

The agitation went on, however, gathering

[1]*American   Supplement—Grove's   Dictionary   of   Music   and Musicians.*

[2]*The Musician*—Nov., 1905—article by A. W. Brayley.

[3]*Dwight's Journal of Music*—Feb. 22, 1873.

strength, one of the tangible results of which was the establishment toward the end of 1832 of the Boston Academy of Music.   This institution became the center of Mr. Mason's teaching activities.   Fifteen hundred pupils, adults, and children were taught the first year.   In addition the Academy carried on an extensive correspondence with educators in many states in the interest of music in the schools.   It thus became known throughout the United States as the national sponsor for music education.   To it should be given credit not only of bringing about the introduction of music into the Boston schools but of making it a live issue in distant states.

In 1836, four years after the first petition, a memorial was prepared by the Academy of Music, endorsed by many prominent citizens, and presented to the School Board.   A special committee of the Board, appointed to consider the memorial, submitted an elaborate and favorable report in 1837.   The historical importance of this report, together with the fact that the arguments brought forward were typical of those used later under similar circumstances by other special committees, make necessary its quotation in full.   The report reads as follows:—
"After mature deliberation and a careful scrutiny of arguments and evidence, the committee are unanimously of opinion that it is expedient to comply with the request of the petitioners.   They are well aware that the cause they support can find no favor

from a board like this except as far as it reaches the convictions through the doors, not of the fancy, but of the understanding."

"Let music be examined by the following standards:—

"1. Intellectually. Music had its place among the seven liberal arts, which scholastic ages regarded as pertaining to humanity. Arithmetic, Geometry, Astronomy, and Music—these formed the quadrivium. Memory, comparison, attention, intellectual faculties—all of them are quickened by a study of its principles. It may be made to some extent a mental discipline.

"2. Morally. It is unphilosophical to say that exercises in vocal music may not be so directed and arranged as to produce those habits of feeling of which these sounds are the type. Happiness, contentment, cheerfulness, tranquillity—these are the natural effects of music.

"3. Physically. It appears self evident that exercise in vocal music, when not carried to an unreasonable excess, must expand the chest and thereby strengthen the lungs and vital organs. Judging then by this triple standard, intellectually, morally, and physically, vocal music seems to have a natural place in every system of instruction which aspires, as should every system, to develop man's whole nature."

"And in regarding the effect of vocal music, as a branch of popular instruction in our schools, there are some practical considerations which in the opinion of your committee are deserving of particular attention."

"Good reading, we all know, is an important object in the present system of instruction in our schools.   And on what does it depend?   Apart from emphasis, on two things mainly, modulation and articulation.   Now modulation comes from the vowel sounds, and articulation from the consonant sounds of the language chiefly.   Dynamics, therefore, or that part of vocal music which is concerned with the force and delivery of sounds, has a direct rhetorical connection.   In fact, the daily sounding of consonant and vowel sounds, deliberately, distinctly, and by themselves, as the committee has heard them sounded in the music lessons given according to the Pestalozzian system of instruction, would, in their opinion, be as good an exercise in the elements of harmonious correct speech as could be imagined.   Roger Ascham, the famous school master and scholar of the Elizabethan era, and surely no mean judge, holds this language:—'All voices, great and small, base and shrill, weak and soft, may be helped and brought to a good point by learning to sing.'   The committee, after observation, confess themselves of this opinion."

"There is another consideration not unworthy of remark: 'Recreation,' says Locke, 'is not being idle, as any one may observe, but easing the weary part by changing of business.' This reflection, in its application to the purposes of instruction, contains deep wisdom. An alternation is needed in our schools, which without being idleness shall yet give rest. Vocal music seems exactly fitted to afford that alternation. A recreation, yet not a dissipation of the mind—a respite, yet not a relaxation,—its office would thus be to restore the jaded energies, and send back the scholars with invigorated powers to other more laborious duties."

"There is one other consideration to which the committee ask the serious attention of the board. It is this:—by the regulations of the school committee it is provided that in all the public schools the day shall open with becoming exercises of devotion. How naturally and how beautifully vocal music would mingle with these exercises; and what unity, harmony and meaning might thus be given to that which, at present, it is feared, is too often found to be a lifeless or an unfruitful service, need only to be suggested to be understood. The committee asks the board to pause, and consider whether the importance has been sufficiently looked to, of letting in a predominant religious sentiment, independently of all forms of faith, to preside over the religious destinies of our schools."

"And now, before proceeding further, let us consider briefly the objections which have been urged against the adoption of vocal music into our system of public schools. It is, then, objected that we aim at that which is impracticable, that singing depends upon a natural ear for music, without which all instruction will be useless. If musical writers and teachers are to be believed, the fact is not so. Undoubtedly in this as in other branches, Nature bestows an aptitude to excel, on different individuals, in very different degrees. Still, what is called a musical ear is mainly the result of cultivation. Mr. Woodbridge has been told by a celebrated music teacher in this country, that out of 4000 pupils not an individual who could not be taught to sing had been found. The ear discriminates sounds as the eye colors. They both may be educated. Early impressions can create an ear for music. It is with learning to sing as with acquiring the pronunciation of a foreign language. Instruction, to be available, must be given while the organs have the flexibility of youth. To learn late in life is generally not to learn at all. There may be cases, it is true, of some who from their earliest years defy efforts of instruction, like those who come into the world maimed in the other senses; they are, however, rare. They are the unfortunate exception to a general rule."

"But it is said, the time spent would be quite inadequate to the end proposed; that the labor of a life is needed to form the musician. The answer to this objection is, that it mistakes the end proposed, which is not to form the musician. Let vocal music, in this respect, be treated like the other branches of instruction. As many probably would be found to excel in music as in arithmetic, writing, or any of the regular studies, and no more. All cannot be orators, nor all poets, but shall we not, therefore, teach the elements of grammar, which orators and poets in common with all others use? It should never be forgotten that the power of understanding and appreciating music may be acquired, where the power of excelling in it is found wanting."

"Again it is objected, if one accomplishment is introduced into the schools, why not another? If instruction is given in vocal music why should it not be given in dancing also? The answer simply is, because music is not dancing: because music has an intellectual character which dancing has not, and above all, because music has its moral purposes which dancing has not. Drawing stands on a very different footing. Drawing, like music, is not an accomplishment merely; it has important uses, and if music be successfully introduced into our public schools, your committee express the hope and conviction that drawing sooner or later will follow."

"The most general objection to the introduction of vocal music is, it will impair discipline. This objection probably had its origin in certain vague impressions of what lessons in vocal music were, when given according to the ancient method of instruction.

The works of Nageli and Pfeiffer, based on the Pestalozzian system and now in general use upon the continent of Europe, were introduced into this country by William Woodbridge. This led to the formation of the Boston Academy of Music. A Manual of vocal music, constructed on the basis of these works, has been prepared by the Professors of this Academy. According to the principles of the Manual, a lesson in vocal music is not unlike a lesson in Arithmetic. Musical takes the place of numerical notation. The blackboard, not the book, is before the pupil, and by the use of his own faculties and senses he goes from principle to principle, till the whole science is evolved. How, then, can an exercise of this kind be adverse to discipline? On the contrary, it is itself a discipline of the highest order, a subordination of mind, eye, and ear unitedly tending to one object, while any deviation from that object is at once made known."

"Vocal music has been adopted as a branch of instruction into some of the most respectable schools in this city. Mr. Thayer, Mr. Fowle, Mr. Haywards, and Messrs. Cushing and Cleveland, have tried it on a limited scale, for different periods of two to four years. Differing in some unessential details, all concur in the main point, the utility of the exercise, and are determined to continue it in their schools."

"Thus tried—tried by the light of reasoning, tried by the objections of its adversaries, tried by the concurrence of attesting witnesses—the introduction of vocal music into the public schools, judged intrinsically, by its effects within and on them, is commended to the favorable consideration of the board."

"What is the great object of our system of popular instruction? Are our schools mere houses of correction, in which animal nature is to be kept in subjection by the law of brute force and the stated drudgery of distasteful tasks? Not so. They have a nobler office. They are valuable mainly as a preparation and a training of the young spirit for usefulness and happiness in coming life. Now, the defect of our present system, admirable as that system is, is this, that it aims to develop the intellectual part of man's nature solely when, for all the true purposes of life, it is of more importance, a hundredfold, to feel rightly than to think profoundly. Besides, human life must and ought to have its amusements. Through vocal music you set in motion a mighty power which silently, but surely, in the end, will humanize, refine and elevate a whole community."

"From this place first went out the great principle, that the property of all should be taxed for the education of all. From this place, also, may the example, in this country, first go forth of that education rendered more complete by the introduction by public authority, of vocal music into our system of popular instruction. The true policy of the American legislator on the subject of education is to gather together whatever good or bright or fair can be found from all countries and all times, and wield the whole for the building up and adorning of the free institutions of our own country."

"If the committee have erred in attaching so much importance to vocal music as a part of public instruction, they can only say they err with Pythagorus, and Plato, Milton and Luther, Pestalozzi, and Fellenberg. Finer spirits than these the world hath not bred. In such company there will be consolation."

"The committee offer the following resolutions:-

"Resolved, that in the opinion of the school committee it is expedient to try the experiment of introducing vocal music, by public authority, as part of the system of public instruction into the public schools of this city."

"Resolved, that the experiment be given in charge to the Boston Academy of Music, under the direction of this board; and that a committee of five be appointed from this board to confer with the Academy, arrange all necessary details of the plan, oversee its operation, and make quarterly report thereof to this board."

"Resolved, that the experiment be commenced as soon as practicable after the passing of these resolutions, and be continued and extended as the board may thereafter determine."

"Resolved, that these resolutions be transmitted to the City Council, and that it be respectfully requested to make such appropriations as may be necessary to carry this plan into effect."[1]

The public school music profession may well feel a thrill of pride and satisfaction in the fact that the sponsors for the introduction of music into the schools voiced their support in a document marked by such lucidity of thought, cogency of reasoning, and nobility of style. On the following 19th of September, 1837, this report was considered and accepted by the school board, and the resolutions as they came from the committee passed, but the city council for some reason failed to grant the expected appropriation which was needed to make the plan operative and give it legal sanction. Whereupon Lowell Mason offered to give his services as teacher of music for a year in one of the schools of the city, and furnish his own books and equipment. This offer was accepted by the board, which in November, 1837, passed the following resolution:—

"Resolved, that in the opinion of the school committee it is expedient that the experiment be tried of introducing instruction in vocal music, by public authority, into the public schools of the city."

"Resolved, that the experiment be tried in the Hawes school in South Boston under the direction

[1]*American History and Cyclopedia of Music—Music in America.* Also *The Early History of Public School Music in the U. S.,* by Frances M. Dickey—M. T. N. A. Proceedings, 1913.

of the sub-committee of that school and the Committee of Music already appointed by this board."

In May of 1838 the Mayor of Boston asked the masters of the Hawes School for a report of the music lessons being given by Lowell Mason. On May 25th they sent him the following letter:—

"Dear sir:—In reply to your communication, allow us briefly to state that any very positive and splendid results from the introduction of vocal music into the Hawes School, cannot yet be reasonably expected, so short has been the time since the first lesson was given, and so interrupted have the lessons been. Still, however, enough has, in our estimation, been already accomplished, to warrant the belief of the great utility of vocal music as a branch of public instruction. One thing has been made evident, that the musical ear is more common than has been generally supposed. There are but few in the school who make palpable discords when all are singing. Many who at the outset of the experiment believed they had neither ear or voice, now sing with confidence and considerable accuracy; and others who could hardly tell one sound from another, now sing the scale with ease;—sufficiently proving that the musical susceptibility is in a good degree improvable. The alacrity with which the lesson is entered upon, and the universal attention with which it is received, are among its great recommendations; they show that the children are agreeably employed; and we are certain that they are innocently employed. We have never known, when, unless extraordinary engagements prevented, they were not glad to remain a half-hour or more, to pursue the exercise after the regular hours of session. They prefer the play of a hard musical lesson to any out-of-door sports; of course understanding that there are some exceptions. Of the great moral effect of vocal music, there can be no question. A song introduced in the middle of the session, has been invariable followed with excellent effect. It is a relief to the wearisomeness of constant study. It excites the listless, and calms the turbulent and uneasy. It seems to renerve the mind, and prepare all for more vigorous intellectual action."

"It is delightful to see how spontaneously a chorus will spring up in any accidental collection of the pupils, about the school house; and how soon five will increase to ten and ten to twenty—all tranquil, yet intensely happy. How much still, refined enjoyment, accompanied as it is with moderate physical exertion, is to be occasionally preferred to constant, boisterous, over-heating, and sometimes dangerous play—with the girls more especially, is this to be desired; for although brisk outdoor exercise is profitable and necessary, yet carried to excess it almost unsexes them, and does them more harm than good. That the music is an attraction is evident from the increased attendance of the pupils on the days of the lessons."

"The advantages to be gained from instructing children in vocal music are of little consequence, when considered in connection with a school, compared with those which are more remote and far less perceptible—such as bear upon their characters, employments, and recreations in after years—upon their condition as social and domestic beings; but with these we have nothing to do."

"This brief notice of the results of so important a step in public education is, we are aware, very insufficient—but we hardly know how to go into details; nor indeed have we time to enter upon an elaborate comment.   We can only thank you, Sir, for the high privilege, which, by your means, we enjoy, in having vocal music taught in our seminary.   We have been equally delighted with the beautiful simplicity of the system upon which Mr. Mason instructs, and with his own personal skill in teaching; and we trust that it will not be long before vocal music will be every where an essential branch of public instruction."

"We are, dear Sir, respectfully

Your obedient servants,

Joseph Harrington, Jr.
John H. Harris
Hawes Hall, May 25, 1838."[1]

[1]*Boston Music Gazette*—Wednesday, July 25, 1838.

We are told that there were exhibitions of the music of the Hawes School from time to time during 1838, and that on August 6 the sub-committee paid the school an official visit and expressed themselves as well satisfied with the excellence of the teaching and the progress of the pupils. On August 14 the annual exhibition of the school took place in the South Baptist Church. The program began with the song *Flowers, Wild Wood Flowers*, which A. W. Brayley says must be recorded as the first ever sung in unison by the pupils of a public school in Boston and probably in this country.[1]

WILD WOOD FLOWERS.

1. Flowers, wild wood flowers ! In a sheltered dell they grew ; I hurried along and I chanced to spy This small star flower with its silvery eye; Then this blue daisy peeped up its head, Sweetly this purple

[1] *The Musician*—Nov., 1905—article by A. W. Brayley.

orchis spread, I gathered them all for you— I

gathered them all for you; All these wild wood flowers, Sweet wild wood

flowers—All these wild wood flowers, Sweet wild wood flowers.

Page from *The Juvenile Singing School,* by Mason and Webb, 1837.

The exhibition was a triumphant demonstration of the suitability of music as a study for children. It attracted a large and critical audience, composed not only of parents, but also of many persons of all sorts who wished to see the results of this novel pedagogical idea of teaching everybody's children to sing. There was prevalent a hard headed incredulity that the thing was impracticable which has not entirely disappeared even today. On August 28, 1838, a fortnight after the exhibition, the school board passed a vote to the effect that the committee on music be instructed to contract with a teacher of vocal music in the several public schools of the city of Boston. In their annual report, July 1, 1839, the Boston Academy of Music, having in mind the long and determined opposition to the musical franchise of the child, referred to the action of the school board not inaptly, as "The Magna Charta of musical education in this country."

Thus after eight years of active legislation, interspersed with petitioning memorials to the school board, followed by favorable action thereon, but always attended by final inaction, was consummated the introduction of music into the public schools of the United States. The significance of the action of August 28, 1838, was not in allowing music to be taught in the schools. It had been allowed and even encouraged for many years, but always by the individual initiative and responsibility of principals and teachers. Its real significance was in the fact that music was included in the curriculum by public authority, like reading, grammar and arithmetic.

Lowell Mason was placed in full charge of the music in the Boston schools with A. N. Johnson, G. F. Root, A. J. Drake, and J. A. Johnson as assistants. Mr. Mason remained in full charge until 1841, when he resigned to devote himself to composing and editing, and carrying forward the work of musical conventions, which necessitated much traveling about the country. His place in the Boston schools was taken by Benjamin F. Baker. The music instruction thus inaugurated was confined to the grammar schools. Music was not taught in the primary grades in an organized way until 1864, when Luther Whiting Mason was appointed to supervise its introduction. High school music was added in 1869 with Julius Eichberg as supervisor, and with the extension of music into all the high schools in 1872 the Boston public school music system became complete.

Chapter III

1838-1861—THE PERIOD OF PIONEERING

MUSIC was established in the Boston Schools in 1838. From that date until the Civil War may be conveniently regarded as the initial introductory period of music in the schools of the country at large. The series of steps which preceded the Boston introduction were more or less faithfully repeated in other cities. Music in the schools was always regarded as an experiment; it had to prove its expediency in each separate instance. It was an untried field, without guiding precedents, except the single Boston experiment and the school-music of Europe, which was little known in this country. There was no school-music profession, and only one Lowell Mason. On the other hand interest in the subject was spreading. The Boston experiment was watched and studied by school men in near and distant states. The Boston Academy of Music worked actively and ceaselessly to prove the suitability and practicability of music as a school subject. The influence of the Academy is shown by the following citation from its annual report of 1835;—"Letters have been received from persons in Georgia,

South Carolina, Virginia, Tennessee, Ohio, Maryland, New York, Connecticut, Vermont, New Hampshire, and Maine, besides many individual societies in Massachusetts asking for information relative to measures which they ought to adopt in order to introduce music as a branch of education into the community where they live."

At the beginning of this period there was little musical culture as we know it today.   Except in Boston, New York, and Philadelphia the people knew nothing of orchestra music.   Chamber music was unknown.   Opera was beginning in New York, but the great day of this expensive luxury was far in the future.   The musical resources of the ordinary town consisted of the church chorus choir, an occasional singing society or town brass band, here and there a private teacher of piano and the singing-school.   People had to travel to the cities to hear good concerts, and these were not plentiful.   Except for the concert advantage, and a greater number of private teachers, the cities were not much better off than the towns.   The Handel and Haydn Society, founded in Boston in 1815, the Germania Orchestra which settled in that city in 1848, and the Mendelssohn Quintet Club which was organized there in 1849, together with the New York Philharmonic Society, organized in 1842 and the Musical Fund Society of Philadelphia were the leading influences in choral and orchestral music in the forties.   There were no conservatories of music, with the single exception of the Boston Academy of Music, which discontinued its work in 1847. But there should be mentioned the fact that this epoch saw the beginning of the rapid development of American instrument manufacturing, especially of pianos, beginning with the Chickering, and also the visits of a considerable number of European artists such as Ole Bull, Sontag, and Thalberg, who toured the country, to which must be added the coming of many musicians from abroad who settled here as teachers.

The full fruition of the ambitions and aspirations implanted in American youth by these various influences did not come for one or more generations. They had one immediate result, however,—that of the pilgrimage to Europe of the American music student, the results of which to American music were not an unmixed good. The prestige of a sojourn in Europe on the part of our music students, and their return home with an attitude of mind colored by foreign traditions, were secondary accompaniments of solid accomplishments necessary to our musical progress, but which marked the beginning of the end of our homogeneous musical life. Up to this time musical cultivation such as there was, was common to all. The musical instructor of all was, and had been for generations, the singing-school. Such culture as could come from learning to sing and read music on the part of old and young of the neighborhoods up and down the land was the product of this home-spun institution. To which must be added to the credit of the singing-school a rather common knowledge of some of the great oratorio music of the world. Thus there existed at this time a wide spread culture in the rudiments of music. This culture was of genuine community caliber, functioning in the home and in social and religious gatherings. But with young America flocking to take lessons of skilled European teachers or of Americans who had returned from abroad, important and necessary as this was for musical culture, there was gradually instilled into the American home an unfortunate feeling of social superiority for solo performance in singing and playing which tended to break down the bonds of social diversion in music, which resulted in a distinct loss in American life, and which the public schools in the present century are attempting to restore.

Public school music, as contemplated by its founder, Lowell Mason, was part of a general educational plan which included every community activity, the school, the church, the choral society, the singing-school and the home. His broad conception of the musical need of the country, and his ability to win others to his point of view, together with his rare skill as a teacher and organizer combined to make the Boston Academy the dominant

CONTENTMENT.

2
The sultan and the grand mogul,
And, what's his name?* who soon,
Though lord of earth, grew very dull
And wistful eyed the moon;
I envy not such men as these,
But laugh at them with perfect ease.

* Alexander the Great.

Page from *The Boston School Song Book,* by Lowell Mason, 1841.

influence in popular music education during this period. It instilled something very like the mission- ary spirit into the teachers whom it prepared, who went forth East and West holding conventions and institutes, working always in the interests of music in the schools, and passing on to their classes the belief in music for everyone, adult and child, which animated them and their great leader.   It is an interesting fact that the culmination of the singing-school movement came during the epoch which introduced music into the schools, and which saw the rise of the private music teacher,—the two influences which more than any other caused it to decline and pass out of existence.

One of the circumstances of the times which retarded artistic progress was the ceaseless westward migration.   With few exceptions the boundary lines of all the future states were laid down before the Civil War, and the majority of them came into statehood during this time.   Our public school system was just emerging from the district school stage.   It was the generation of the Webster speller and the Coburn arithmetic.   The frame work of the American school system, its division into primary, intermediate, grammar and high schools, existed already in New England, and was being gradually adopted by the other states.   It was this generation which settled, by strenuous agitation, the principle of free, non-sectarian, tax-supported and state-controlled schools.   This epoch, in which Horace Mann, Henry Barnard, and Caleb Mills battled for recognition of the school as the nation's greatest asset, probably gave more attention to discussion of public education than any other period of our history. The nation was young, rich in latent possibilities, but not wealthy in fact, and adequate appropriations for schools were not yet taken as a matter of course. The children studied reading, writing, arithmetic, geography and grammar; and the separation of the pupils into grades from the first to the ninth grade with a teacher for each grade, which first occurred during this period, called attention to the importance of training teachers, and led to the establishment of Normal schools. The prevailing type of secondary school was still the academy, and the development of the high school was only just beginning.

In the promotion of public education in the West, Ohio took a leading part, and the influence of Cincinnati in this region became very similar to that of Boston in the East. "As early as 1832 Calvin E. Stowe, who afterwards married Harriet Beecher, was appointed as special investigator into methods of education in public schools, and was sent to Europe to study the educational systems of Germany, France and England. He made his report in 1836. The report was very comprehensive and included the following paragraphs with regard to the use of vocal and instrumental music in the schools of Germany.—

"The universal success and very beneficial results with which the arts of drawing and designing, vocal and instrumental music, moral instruction and the Bible have been introduced into the schools was another fact peculiarly interesting to me—I asked all the teachers with whom I conversed, whether they did not sometimes find children who were actually incapable of learning to draw and to sing.

"I have had but one reply, and that was that they found the same diversity of natural talent in regard to these as in regard to writing, reading and other branches of education, but they had never seen a child that was capable of learning to read and write who could not be taught to sing well and to draw neatly, and that, too, without taking any time which would at all interfere with, indeed which would not actually promote his progress in other subjects."

"This report was also presented to the Massachusetts legislature, where it had great influence in giving public school music, which had already been introduced into the Boston schools, a more secure footing, and resulted in many other Massachusetts cities introducing music."[1]   It certainly helped greatly to place music in the school of Cincinnati and Cleveland and perhaps also those of Chicago and Pittsburgh.

There is uncertainty regarding some of the dates which mark the introduction of music into the cities which followed the example of Boston.   The

[1] C. H. Miller—*Music in the Grade Schools*—M. T. N. A. Proceedings, 1920.

most available data are contained in the valuable
paper by Frances M. Dickey on *The Early History
of Public School Music in the United States*.   Quoting from Miss Dickey's paper, they are as follows;—
"Buffalo, 1843; Pittsburgh, 1844; Cincinnati, 1846;
Chicago, 1848; Cleveland, 1851; San Francisco,
1851; and St. Louis, 1852."   The widely scattered
locations of these cities and the comparatively short
interval between the earliest and the latest, indicate
that such interest as there was in the introduction of
music was a part of the general educational thought
of the period.   To these dates may be added that of
Providence in 1848, which is mentioned by Cubberley.[1]
Regarding the Cincinnati date, a pamphlet written
in memory of Charles Aiken states that "Music was
introduced into the Cincinnati schools in 1845, the
music teacher in charge being Wm. F. Coburn.   Mr.
Aiken became his successor in 1848."   In an article
in *School Music* of January, 1913, E. L. Baker states
that in 1840 a music teacher was employed in the
Chicago schools at a salary of $16.00 per month.
Caroline B. Bourgard claims that Louisville introduced music in 1844, the same year as Pittsburgh,
thus tying with that city for third place in the introduction roll.   In an article in *School Music* of
November, 1914 she quotes from the minutes of the
Louisville board of education to support her statement.

[1]Ellwood P. Cubberley—*Public Education in the United States*—
  Houghton, Mifflin & Company, 1919, page 252.

The article also quotes from the minutes of 1852, regarding the employment of two music teachers. This, on account of the future importance of one of them, would have a place here.   "Two gentlemen, L. W. Mason and Wm. Fallen, Esq., have been highly recommended as efficient and successful professors of music.   As both gentlemen are highly recommended and as it is advisable to secure for our schools the very best instruction possible and as experience alone can enable the Board of Trustees to determine which of the two gentlemen is the best adapted to the work, your committee would recommend that both gentlemen be employed for three months to teach vocal music in the six grammar schools of this city, each taking three schools.   That two lessons of one hour each be given in each school per week and that compensation for their services be allowed at the rate of $25 per month and that this engagement be entered into with the understanding that at the expiration of three months an examination shall be held of the several schools by persons whom the Board of Trustees may appoint and that in case either of the gentlemen shall decline accepting the appointment the other shall take charge of the six schools and receive compensation at the rate of $50 per month."

The sequel follows.   From the minutes Feb. 14, 1853;—

"The committee appointed by your Board to investigate and determine between the relative merits of Messrs. Fallen and Mason by an examination of their pupils would report viz:—

"That after an impartial and candid examination and in connection with the counsel of several eminent musical gentlemen your committee is unable to decide with any unanimity in favor of one to the exclusion of the other. Both teachers in the opinion of your committee have rendered faithful and effective services. Under such circumstances your committee deems it unjust to rule off either. It would therefore recommend that both teachers be employed with such changes in amount of salary and employment as would render it an object for them to continue and for the Board to employ them. Your committee is further induced to this recommendation by the warm if not enthusiastic interest which the people manifested on the occasion of the examination of both teachers."

From the records of the Columbia Historical Society of New York we learn that music was introduced into the schools of Washington, D. C., in 1845, while the Lancastrian system was in full sway. The first teacher of vocal music was J. H. Hewitt. He was followed in 1856 by Joseph H. Daniel. Mr. Daniel's services extended over a period of more than forty years. In 1865, when the veteran armies of the Union marched past the Capitol, to be reviewed by President Lincoln, General Grant, and the other generals who had commanded them, a chorus of 2500 children sang *The Star Spangled Banner, Battle Cry of Freedom,* and other patriotic songs under Mr. Daniel's direction.

As early as 1836, attempts were made in New York City to have vocal music as a regular branch of instruction in the schools, which were at that time maintained by the Public School Society, a semi-philanthropic institution, whose funds came from various religious denominations, and which was given an annual grant of money by the state. The matter of music instruction was left to the direction of the various schools, with the understanding that no expense should be incurred by the Society. Numerous similar attempts were made from time to time. Dissension in the Public School Society regarding the division of State funds among certain denominational schools caused the New York State Legislature in 1842 to create the New York City Board of Education, thus doing away with all sectarian religious domination of the schools. From this time music undoubtedly began to have a place in the schools of New York City, and in 1854 George F. Bristow, well known as a violinist and composer, was appointed visiting teacher of music, in which capacity he continued to serve until his death in 1898. In that year, 1898, music became definitely included in the curriculum of the New York City school system, at which time Frank Damrosch was placed in charge of the work.

In 1860 a special committee on music of the Philadelphia Board of Controllers submitted a report, quoting in full the Boston Committee report of 1837, and ending with the following resolution:—
"Resolved, that the Council be requested to make an appropriation to furnish each of the Grammar Schools of the First District with pianofortes, and a teacher whose duty it shall be to give half-hour lessons in singing twice a week, to the pupils in said schools."

The following paragraphs are supplied through the courtesy of Paul E. Duffield, of Philadelphia, who has written a thesis upon the development of public school music in that city.

"The first mention of music in any public school of Philadelphia occurs in the first report of the Principal of the Normal School, dated August 29, 1848. The departments of instruction at that time are listed as follows:— Theory and Practice of Teaching; Mathematics; History; Grammar; Reading; Drawing and Writing; Music. The list of regular faculty members included the name of Mr. D. F. Alden, Instructor in Vocal Music. The total enrollment of the school numbered 106 pupils and the Principal states further that 'The language of the plan of the school defines the object of instruction to be the thorough training of the pupils in the branches taught in Public Schools, with reference to teaching them.'

"Mr. Alden was succeeded the following year by Mr. George Kingsley, who held the position until 1851. During this period the records indicate that there were five daily recitations in the Normal School, besides the exercises in Drawing, Penmanship, and the Elements and Practice of Vocal Music. William E. Fenney next occupied this position for two years at an annual salary of $150, giving way in 1854 to John Bower, whose salary was then increased to $300. The next incumbent, Thomas Bishop, taught for two years (1857-1858) and was replaced by Mary H. Henderson (1859-1864) whose salary had reached $400, when she was succeeded by Professor Cornelius Everest. Professor Everest was an immediate success and the Principal's report for the school term (1865-1866) devotes an extensive paragraph to the flourishing condition of vocal music, which was then taught to all pupils in the school, divided into three separate classes.

"Meanwhile sporadic efforts at musical instruction in the primary schools must have cropped out from time to time, since in the Controller's Report to the Board of Education on December 31, 1864, this very significant statement occurs: 'Vocal music is taught at the expense of the pupils, when taught at all. This is a departure from the liberal principles involved in our school system. A small annual appropriation for the payment of a few music teachers would not materially increase our expenditures.   One teacher may instruct in vocal music four schools per day, twenty schools per week; and thus with four or five music teachers all the Grammar Schools may be instructed to a moderate degree in vocal music.'   However, nothing further is to be found as a result of this recommendation during the ensuing four years, although Professor Everest continued to hold his position, in what had now become the Girls' High and Normal School, with consistent success and at a gradually increasing salary."

To the list of places known to have introduced music between 1838 and 1852 may be added a few others, as indicated in the following citations from the report of the school committee of Worcester, Massachusetts, of 1854.   It contains several points of interest.   "Special inquiry has recently been made by the Committee, to ascertain to what extent the practice of singing is carried on in our schools. They learn with pleasure that in all of them except suburban schools, vocal music is habitually practiced. In many of these, however, it is not taught, nor is the teacher always able to participate in the exercise. The result is that in many classes, the pupils acquire inaccurate habits of singing, and these prove very hard to remove.   Besides this, there are always children who might take part, but do not, for want of instruction, and thus an exercise which all might share, is confined to one-half or two-thirds.

"But why should not vocal music be taught in

our schools as systematically as loud reading?   It affords quite as much discipline to thought and taste, —it is more likely to be a source of pleasure in later years,—and nothing has a more refining or harmonizing influence.   In the Boston grammar schools, (which include the grade of our elementary schools also) singing is taught by professional teachers, during two half-hours of every week.   We give also the experience of other cities.

"Charlestown, (report of 1849)—'Vocal music has been taught in the high and grammar schools, by a skillful teacher and with good success.   We hope it may be continued as a branch of common education, for the healthful influence it exerts upon the discipline of the schools, and for its happy and lasting effects upon the character of the pupils.'

"Lowell, (report of 1849)—'Two lessons of half an hour each, are given each week to the grammar schools and to the two departments of the high school. There is but one opinion among those competent to judge, of the success of the experiment that has been tried.   The influence of the music lessons on the pupils is pleasing and salutary, and the proficiency that has been made, and the accuracy that has been attained, are creditable to all concerned.'

"Lynn, (report of 1852)—'One important improvement, which we have introduced, is that of instruction in music. Upon scarcely any measure have the committee been so fully agreed as upon this.

The experiment has answered all reasonable expectations. The committee, after witnessing the exhibition in music at the examinations of the schools, were clear in the conviction that this process of instruction should be continued.'

"Cambridge, (report of 1852)—'One of the most interesting matters connected with the examination was the singing. When we say, that we were at once charmed by the melody we listened to, and convinced that the City wisely spends the amount appropriated for the salary of the teacher of music, we are confident that every parent, every individual who attended the examination, will give us credit for sincerity. It is indeed highly gratifying to notice the proficiency already gained by many of the pupils, and believing as the committee do, that nearly every scholar can learn to sing, as well as to read, we trust that this branch of education will continue to receive the fostering care of the City.' "

If we regard the report from which quotations have been made as reflecting the general status of music in the schools, three important inferences may be drawn from it:—

1. Singing was quite generally practiced in the schools before its formal introduction by public authority, and often with excellent results.

2. Whenever music was formally introduced a special music teacher was appointed, thus making music a special subject.

3.   This special teacher was not a supervisor. He was the authorized school music teacher.   The Boston school board report of 1836 distinctly stated that the music teaching shall be under the supervision of the sub-committee of the board.   The evolution of the special music teacher into the supervisor of music came much later.   It is a plain inference, also, that though the regular teacher might conduct the song singing of the children, the special music teacher was expected to teach not only singing but music reading.   The evolution which made the regular teacher responsible for her own music teaching came very gradually and at a later period.

It is worthy of note that the introductory period of school-music was inspired by lofty aims and unselfish purposes, the sort of aims and purposes which call for a fine type of leadership.   The same vision which inspired Horace Mann and Henry Barnard in general education, inspired Lowell Mason, Charles Aiken and others in music.   It led them to give themselves unstintedly to the new cause, and frequently without remuneration.   Lowell Mason gave his services in Boston in 1837-1838, and Charles Aiken worked for a year in the Cincinnati schools, 1842-1843, without salary.[1]   The same is true of W. G. Van Meter in Louisville in 1846,[2] and of Amos Whiting in Worcester, Mass., in 1861.   When school

[1]Letter from Walter H. Aiken to the author.
[2]Caroline B. Bourgard in *School Music*—Nov., 1914.

boards were hesitating to introduce music, and were uncertain as to its practicability, a voluntary demonstration of its educational value often turned the scale.

The basis of remuneration of music teachers at this early state was varying and uncertain. In the cities regular salaries were the rule, ranging, according to the Boston School Board Report of 1858, from $400 to $1350. In all places, cities and towns included, the salary was reckoned by the lesson, by the month, by the term, or by the year, as the case might be. In the towns $300 a year, $100 a term, $16 a month and one dollar for an hour's lesson are some of the modest salaries known to have been paid. On the whole, however, the remuneration for music teachers was probably equal to that of other teachers for the same amount of work.

It would be mere guess work to try to estimate the number of music introductions prior to the Civil War. As already stated, there was more or less singing of a sort under the guidance of the regular teachers. The question was not that of allowing singing in the schools; it was that of employing a special teacher to have charge of the singing, and to teach music reading. The larger cities, with their more ample funds, centrally controlled schools and educational leadership initiated and led the movement, and the nearby communities, influenced by the example of the cities, followed as soon as circumstances permitted.　Starting with the list of cities already given which introduced music between 1838 and 1852, and, allowing for as many more unknown places for the same period, a total of twenty-eight, it would be over liberal to estimate the number of introductions between 1838 and the Civil War as more than fifty.

The first teachers of public school music as well as the methods of teaching came directly from the singing-school.　The public school music class was, in fact, a transplanted singing-school.　Even the books were in many cases the same, though juvenile song collections prepared for children's classes were soon plentiful.　They had the same oblong shape as the traditional tune-book, but were of smaller dimensions, so that the *Carmina Sacra* and the *Golden Wreath* suggested respectively the older and younger members of the same musical family.

The methods of the singing-school needed little or no change when transferred to the public school. The music teacher during this period gave lessons only in the grammar and high schools, and these children were mature enough themselves to attend singing-schools, and doubtless many of them did. There was, to be sure, the important difference that now all the children were to be taught singing instead of the talented few.　Morever, in this epoch children went to school to get knowledge, which meant book knowledge.　This theory of education was applied to music as well as to all other subjects. The children were taught the elements of music, they became familiar with the notes, and they learned to read music. The generous length of the music lesson, a half-hour and sometimes more, and the fact that the lesson was always given by a special teacher fully accounts for that fact. It is worthy of record that public school music in these early days, at least, fully vindicated the expectations of its advocates, and all the available contemporary testimony regarding it points to the conclusion that music was taught at least as well as the other subjects, and in many cases, far better.

Of the pioneer public school music teachers, the most striking figure with the exception of Lowell Mason, was Charles Aiken of Cincinnati. His influence went far beyond his own state of Ohio, and his distinctive position among the pioneers was that of the ideal music teacher, unselfish and devoted, loving his subject and beloved by his pupils. He came to Cincinnati in 1842, having graduated from Dartmouth College. Until his official connection with the schools in 1848, with the exception of a year's gratuitous teaching, his energies were directed to working out a system of instruction in his adult music classes, using the movable Do. These years established his leadership in both city and state. Personal integrity, high scholarship, a passion for thoroughness, and the ability to stand on his own feet, to think things out for himself, were all factors in this influence.   He edited for use in the elementary schools a series of music books known as *The*

CHARLES AIKEN
(Memorial bust in Music Hall, Cincinnati, Ohio)

Cincinnati Music Readers, and for the high schools *The High School Choralist* and *The Choralist's Companion.*   These books, remarkable for their time, were filled with choice selections of the great masters. Nourished by choral works of this kind, and taught for more than thirty years by a man who radiated their spirit, the children of Cincinnati grew up with an appreciation of music which has become a tradition. The resulting harvest from the seed thus constantly sown and cultivated is a music loving city, supporting a great biennial festival, of which choruses of children form an integral part, a symphony orchestra, and colleges of music of the first rank, the whole forming a community enterprise, with its foundations firmly laid in music in the schools.

Cincinnati also has the distinction of being the first city to introduce musical instruction in the primary grades in 1857, when Luther Whiting Mason came from Louisville to teach in that city. This development, however, belongs to the next period.

Another pioneer, whose record of service covered the long span of fifty-two years, was William A. Hodgdon, of St. Louis. He studied with Lowell Mason and George J. Webb, and came from New Hampshire to St. Louis in 1854. How he started his work was described many years ago in an article in the *St. Louis Globe-Democrat* on old school-times. "There was not at first the slightest preparation for music teaching in any of the city schools. There were no music books, no instruments; Mr. Hodgdon had to furnish everything out of his head, and did so. Selecting a song suitable to the capacity of the pupils, he wrote the words upon the blackboard and

WILLIAM A. HODGDON

sang them over stanza by stanza until the children had memorized both words and melody, a system, which, Mr. Hodgdon believes, will develop, to a greater extent than any other, the musical tastes of the young, prior to the systematic instruction in notation. The first music book in the high school was Lowell Mason's *Song Garden,* which in time, was followed by the *School Companion,* and almost contemporaneously Mr. Hodgdon introduced the *Golden Wreath* in the grammar schools."

Mention has been made of the fact that the early school music teachers were singing-school teachers also. W. S. B. Mathews, the eminent piano pedagogue and editor, when a young man, at one time fulfilled the duties of choir director and organist, singing-school teacher and convention leader, private piano teacher and public school music teacher. How he managed such a many-sided occupation is graphically shown in a letter which he wrote to *Dwight's Journal of Music* in 1859, describing a typical week's work.

"Perhaps some of your readers may like to know something of a music teacher's life 'out West.' For the edification of such I subjoin a memorandum of a week's work of a music teacher in regular standing.

"Monday—Take the cars at ten o'clock and go to B., 13 miles, 10 by railroad and 3 by stage. In P. M. give private lessons from 2 to 4 on melodeon. Eve., singing class numbering 75. They will sing the Cantata *Daniel* at the close of the course as a concert.

"Tuesday—9 to 10 A. M. singing lesson to public school. P. M. 2 private lessons. Eve., singing class at C., (3 miles from B) numbering 50. The weekly singing-school is an event to most of them and the enthusiasm is proportionately great.

"Wednesday—One private lesson. Eve., singing class, numbering 70, at D, (5 miles from C). The enthusiasm is good, and they will sing *Esther*, by Bradbury, at close of the course.

"Thursday—Take the cars at 3 A. M. and go to E., 17 miles from D, (we came back to D after singing-school last eve.) and give private lessons on pianoforte all day, say ten lessons. Return to A on the cars. This evening, for a wonder, we have to ourself, and luxuriate in going to bed at 8 P. M.

"Friday—Give 4 private lessons on piano. At 1 P. M. lesson to public school one hour. Eve., choir meeting; this is a Catholic choir, and sing Mozart's Masses and such like. This evening is a pleasure.

"Saturday—Take the cars at 7 A. M., go to B,

7 miles, and walk to F, 3 miles further on.   Give 6
piano lessons, return to A, and sing at the choir
rehearsal (Baptist) from 7.30 to 8.30.   At 8.30 go
to Catholic choir, and return home at 11 P. M.
thoroughly tired both in mind and body.   You retire
to rest with the comfortable consciousness of being
able to sleep until 8 o'clock the next A. M.

"Sunday—At 10.30 A. M. go to Baptist church
and play and conduct for first 2 hymns, which being
got along with, must be at Catholic mass at 11 A. M.
This lasts until 1 o'clock, and then hurrah for
freedom until 4 o'clock when Vespers require our attention.   This is soon over, and we are free again
until 5.30 P. M., when evening service at Baptist
must be attended.   Finally at 9 o'clock P. M., your
week's work may be summed up at 28 private lessons,
3 singing classes, 2 public school lessons, 3 choir
meetings, and 4 services on Sunday.   Sometimes
this routine is varied by an application to conduct
a 3 days' session of some county musical convention,
when we delight in the best of Psalmody, anthems,
and choruses from Mozart and Handel.

" 'What works do we use?'   Why, for singing
classes on Monday and Tuesday eve., the *Shawm*,
Wednesday eve., the *Jubilee;* in the public schools,
Mason's *Normal Singer;* for the melodeon, Zundel's
Method; for the pianoforte, Richardson's *New
Method*, which we like much; for advanced pupils,
anything from Gobel to Beethoven.

"Does it pay? Well, pretty well; here is the tariff. Private lessons 50 cents each; public school, one dollar each; singing classes for 12 lessons, one dollar per scholar. Conventions any where form $25 to $100 for 3 days. The first sum is about the customary price to a local conductor. Choirs $100 per annum each.

"Is there much musical taste here? Well, yes, at least for the country which is so new. We have some fine musicians in the West.

"A good knowledge of music, geniality, good humor, knowledge of human nature and 'soft sawder,' and untiring energy are essential to succeed here, and with them one may do well, as the above (which is the actual week's work of the writer) will show."[1]

The above letter is instructive in several respects. It shows that just before the Civil War there was plenty of musical interest in this western country, and that the singing-school and convention were in vogue. It indicates also that pianos were numerous, and the melodeon had not yet become a curiosity. The writer, W. S. B. Mathews, is a rather exceptional but perfectly typical example of a self-made American musician, who learned by thinking and working, always busy doing the next thing needed to be done. In his youth he came under the influence of Lowell Mason, and afterward collaborated with William

[1] *Dwight's Journal of Music;* Dec. 24, 1859.

Mason, his son, in editing works on piano instruction, besides writing voluminous works on music history and appreciation. As musical critic on one of the Chicago papers, and as editor and publisher of the magazine *Music*, he exerted a healthful influence upon musical progress in the last decades of the nineteenth century.

We have somewhat arbitrarily taken the years between 1838 and 1860 as the introductory period of public school music. For some reasons it might also include the decade after the Civil War. During this epoch the most fundamental questions relating to American education were discussed and settled. It was settled that the schools would be free to all, that they should be tax supported, free from all church interference, and that they should be controlled by the state. Though the number of cities and towns introducing music was not very large, the importance of the cities taking this step, and the good results of their teachers, especially in Boston and Cincinnati, gave the subject a prestige which helped to accelerate the movement. There was no school-music profession as yet, and the music teachers were isolated each from the other. They met their associate singing-school teachers and choir leaders, however, at the numerous musical conventions, where the subject was constantly agitated and talked about. The common agencies of popular music education were still the singing-school, the convention, and the normal institute, and in the West, especially, these three institutions continued to flourish vigorously for several decades after the Civil War.

NOTE: Too late for insertion in its place on page 65, information has come from William Breach, director of music in the schools of Buffalo, that he has discovered the date of the introduction of music into the Buffalo schools to have been 1837, as is shown in the records of the school board.

CHAPTER IV

THE BEGINNINGS OF METHOD
(1861-1885)

IN a certain sense the real beginnings of public school music came after the Civil War. The early introductions were relatively few and were confined mainly to the cities where the schools were under the control of a single school board. Before the War and for a decade thereafter, the prevailing type of school control throughout the country was the district school system, with each district of a town managing its own school affairs, levying its own school taxes, and through its board of three trustees selecting its own teachers. Under such conditions music introductions did not come as a matter of course. Before music could become a school subject it had to win the approval of the voters of the district, not, to be sure, at the polls, but nevertheless at the bar of public opinion. And with those who had musical talent able to find instruction in the ubiquitous singing-school, the average man did not feel it the duty of the district to provide such teaching for every child. This may account in part for the fact that as late as 1886, Gen. John Eaton, United States

Commissioner of Education reported that less than 250 school systems were regularly teaching music.

Agitation on the subject went on persistently, however, and the marked advance in every direction of the general field of music helped to give it impetus. Some aspects of this progress should be given attention at this point.

First may be mentioned the rapid rise to the level of a recognized profession of the private music teacher. The enormous growth in the number of private teachers came partly as the result of the stimulus toward musical culture given by the singing-schools, but it was greatly accelerated by the desire of thousands of talented young people to become solo performers. The concerts of great European artists fired the ambition of our youth, an ambition which was intensified by the successes on the concert stage of native Americans like Adelaide Phillips, Annie Louise Carey, Clara Louise Kellogg, William Mason and William H. Sherwood. A significant evidence of the growing influence of the private teacher in musical progress was the organization in 1876 of the Music Teachers National Association.

Secondly, there was wide spread choral activity distinguished by high artistic aims, marked by the formation of numerous choral clubs and societies such as the Apollo Club of Chicago and the Oratorio Society of New York. The same fact is illustrated in the music festivals which were given both in the

West and in the East.   The great Boston Peace Jubilees of 1869, with a chorus of 10,000 and an orchestra of 1000, and of 1872 with double that number of participants, were chiefly remarkable for the gigantic nature of the enterprises, though the sheer achievement of bringing together from far and near singing societies and choirs on such a scale of magnitude makes these occasions unique in our history.   The Cincinnati Biennial Festival and the Boston Handel and Haydn Triennial are examples of the same activity on a much higher plane.

Thirdly, the formation of symphony orchestras such as the Theodore Thomas Orchestra, the Symphony Society of New York, and the Boston Symphony Orchestra gave multitudes the opportunity of hearing faultless renditions of instrumental works, an opportunity of the utmost importance to well rounded musical development.

A parallel movement of even more immediate influence upon the generality of people was the large number of excellent regimental and concert bands which appeared after the Civil War under such leaders as Gilmore, Reeves and Brooks, to which may be added the fact that the highly versatile bands maintained by such huge traveling shows as P. T. Barnum's were heard annually by millions.

Fourthly, the rather rapid development of music in colleges and the establishment of independent conservatories of music such as the New England Conservatory and the Cincinnati Conservatory.

The combined effect of this four-fold influence upon general musical culture was very great. It raised the whole general interest in music to a higher level; it brought into existence a distinct musical profession, consisting of teachers, concert performers, and critics, together with a multitude of listeners of every degree of critical appreciation. And it paved the way slowly but inexorably for the introduction of music into all the public schools.

The opportunities increasingly offered during this period for music lessons in the grammar and high schools, and for study with private teachers, and the beginning of the vogue of the quartet choir with paid soloists, all combined to take away from the singing-schools their former clientele, with the result that they began to lose ground. The decline of the singing-school led also to the decline of the convention and the normal institutes. Many of the latter became permanent conservatories of music. The causes which brought these institutions to an end developed only gradually, however, and they still continued in certain localities, especially in the Mississippi states where they did an effective work for many years.

In public education the development of the period was in the direction of the well trained teacher. Teaching rose to the level of an art and a skilled profession. The spirit of Pestalozzi became its ruling force. Subject matter and text books were written and rewritten to conform to the new ideals. Private and public normal schools multiplied rapidly and trained thousands of students in the theory and practice of teaching. The feeling of need for trained teachers was so keen that many cities began to maintain training schools of their own. With the rise to new dignity of the teaching profession came also the office of superintendent of schools as the executive head of the system. The supervisory idea thus initiated was later applied to departments and subjects, resulting in the appointing of supervising principals and supervisors of special branches. The new standard of teaching was fostered and strengthened by the formation of the National Education Association in 1857 and many state associations.

The addition of the primary school below the intermediate school, which completed the structure of the American school system, with its primary, intermediate, grammar and high school divisions made evident the need of a method of music instruction which should articulate all the grades under one plan. The accomplishment of this task was largely the work of Luther Whiting Mason. He belonged to a distant branch of Lowell Mason's family, and was one of his pupils. But before considering Mr. Mason's career it may be well to review that of a few other teachers who began their work in this

LUTHER WHITING MASON

BENJAMIN JEPSON

WALTER H. AIKEN

NATHAN L. GLOVER

N. COE STEWART

GEORGE B. LOOMIS

EMMA THOMAS SUMMER SCHOOL, DETROIT, MICHIGAN, 1892.
NATIONAL SUMMER SCHOOL.

period. The first of these is Benjamin Jepson of New Haven, Connecticut.

Before the Civil War Mr. Jepson had been very successful in training choruses of children. This work was always done out of school hours. He came to believe that the work he had been doing should have a place in the public schools and that the schools should teach the children to read music. After his return from service in the Union Army in 1865 Mr. Jepson persuaded the school board of New Haven to "try the experiment" of introducing music into the schools. The experiment was tried; Mr. Jepson was placed in charge, and during his service of fifty years the music in the New Haven schools was preeminently successful. The following is his own account of how he began the work:—

"On the 3rd of January, 1865, I entered upon my duties, having in charge the upper rooms of seven school houses, numbering about 1200 pupils. Year by year more schools, rooms, and pupils were added, until all from kindergarten to high were included. I found at once a plentiful lack of apparatus with which to commence the work of elementary instruction. No grade music books or charts, no staff-lined black boards, less than a half dozen pianos or instruments of any description, and only a scanty supply of books containing hymns for devotional exercises. Most assuredly the outlook was forbidding. The school principals had no particular sympathy with the new branch of study, but were willing that the experiment should be tried.   The regular teachers also, a majority of whom had little or no knowledge of musical theory, seemed willing that I should succeed, providing success did not involve additional labor for them.   The board of education simply acquiesed in the proposition and appointed one of their number· to confer with me in reference to the general plan of instruction.   The plan of most of our school houses at that time was a two story building containing six rooms on each floor, with a hall twenty feet wide running the entire length of the building.   The gentleman appointed by the board of education advised that we proceed with caution, doing nothing to antagonize the views of the teachers or to excite public opposition.   He suggested as a general plan that during certain hours of certain days, the pupils of the six upper rooms without reference to grade, might file into these long halls and remain standing during the exercises, say fifteen or twenty minutes, while I as precenter and vocal instructor occupied one end of the hall."

"As you may well understand the first lesson of this kind did not accord with my plans of methodical instruction in the science of music.   It was only after a vigorous protest that I succeeded in convincing all concerned on the utter absurdity of such a waste of time and energy.   It was difficult indeed to convince the authorities that the pupils should remain in their session rooms, and that musical instruction should be governed by the same rules and regulations as obtained in other studies."

"In the absence of all other musical apparatus, I had constructed at my own expense, a musical chart

EXERCISES FOR IMITATION.

Practice by syllable and word, teacher and class alternating.
Place the following exercises on the blackboard, teacher pointing as class sings.

EXERCISES.

13 Do on added line.

Do Mu - sic floats, Soft - est notes.

14 Do on added line.

Do Sun-shine bright, Gives us light.

15 Do in space below.

Do Love - ly May, Come and stay.

16 Do in space below.

Do Birds in air, Free from care.

17 Do on first line.

Do Flow - ers fair, Scent the air.

18 Do on first line.

Do Voic - es chime, Keep - ing time.

19 Do in first space.

Do Fount-ains flow, Murm'ring low.

20 Do in first space.

Do Hol - i - day, Time for play

21 Do on second line.

Do Come with me, You shall see.

22 Do on second line.

Do Sweet - ly sing, Birds of Spring.

23 Do in second space.

Do Now we go, To and fro.

24 Do in second space.

Do Half past eight, Don't be late.

25 Do on third line.

Do Dark - est night, Stars shine bright.

26 Do on third line.

Do Close of day, Haste a - way.

27 Do on added line.

Do Sil - ver moon, Calm looks down.

28 Do on added line.

Do Work is done, Now for fun.

Page from *New Standard Music Reader, First and Second Years*, by Benjamin Jepson; The Tuttle, Morehouse & Taylor Company.
(By courtesy of Prof. Harry B. Jepson.)

containing upwards of 1200 square feet of canvas. This chart was hung on a portable frame and reeled off with a crank.   With this contrivance transported from school to school in a wagon, I commenced the work of musical instruction in the New Haven public schools.   I soon wore out my musical hurdy-gurdy; in the meantime I prepared and published at my own expense, the first book in the United States known as a *Music Reader*.   In order to keep pace with the increased interest in sight reading, and at the same time to stimulate progress, I have found it necessary at intervals of ten years to revise the original work, first with a series of three books, then four books and finally six books now in use."

"At the end of the first year, I obtained the privilege of a public rehearsal of school-music methods in the largest hall in the city.   The mayor of the city presided, the stage was occupied by the board of education, representatives of the press, the clergy and other prominent citizens; the entire lower floor was filled with delegates from all the grades and schools; the galleries were filled with parents and friends of the children.   The exercises included sight singing by individuals and classes from the blackboard, interspersed with rote songs.   The impression made was deep and lasting.   Voluminous reports in the newspapers commended me for the results of musical instruction in the schools, with now and then a newspaper article from a disgruntled

tax payer. I may say from that day to the present
the trend of public sentiment has been steadily upward. The children who participated in that demonstration are the fathers and mothers of the present
generation, not only of pupils, but of a majority of
the teachers of New Haven."[1]

Yale University conferred upon Benjamin Jepson the honorary degree of Master of Arts in 1912.
In conferring this degree President Hadley paid
him the following tribute:—"The crowning achievement of his life has been to introduce music as a
regular study in our public schools. As one of the
earliest musical supervisors in the school system of
America, he became a national figure." The same
year, 1912, the School Board of New Haven honored
Mr. Jepson by naming for him one of the schools.

Another leading supervisor of the period was
George B. Loomis, who in 1866 began teaching music
in the schools of Indianapolis, having been recommended for this position by Lowell Mason. As was
the case with Mr. Jepson, he started with little or
no materials for instruction, used his initiative and
resourcefulness in working out his methods in the
school room, and then published his system of teaching in a series of books under the title of *Loomis'
Progressive Music Lessons*. The method proceeded
by very careful steps to develop the tones of the scale
and the elements of simple rhythm. It began with

[1] Address before the Music Supervisors National Conference, 1910.

FIRST STEPS IN MUSIC.

No. 72.

PAPA'S WATCH.

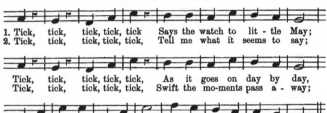

1. Tick,   tick,   tick, tick, tick   Says the watch to   lit - tle   May;
2. Tick,   tick,   tick, tick, tick,   Tell me what it   seems to   say;

Tick,   tick,   tick, tick, tick,   As it   goes on   day by   day,
Tick,   tick,   tick, tick, tick,   Swift the mo-ments pass a - way;

It will nei-ther stop nor stay,   All the night and all   the   day.
Waste them not, but   try   to   learn;—Moments past can ne'er re - turn.

No. 73.

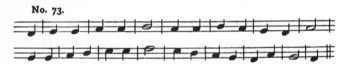

You will observe that the above exercise begins with the *last* part of the measure, or the *upward beat*. Begin after *three beats*, as, *down, up, down*, and with the *upward* beat sing the first tone. *With which part of the measure does the exercise begin?* (Second.) *With which beat?* (Upward.)

No. 74.

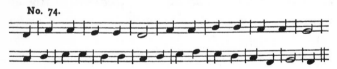

Page from *Progressive Music Lessons, First Book,*
by George B. Loomis.   American Book Company, publishers.

a one-line staff, then added another line, then another,
and so on until the five line staff was complete.   The

simplicity of singing-school methods was applied and adapted to the ability of small children. There were careful directions for the grade teacher, and the books were widely used in Indiana and the neighboring states during the seventies and eighties. Mr. Loomis was a widely known music teacher. He was a charter member of the Indiana Music Teachers Association, which was formed in 1877, one of the first of such associations. His personality and character were such that superintendent Shortridge said of him,—"It is not every city that is so fortunate as to have found a MAN as well as a teacher of music."

Some others who were prominent figures in school-music in the Middle West and who began their work soon after the Civil War were Milton Z. Tinker, of Evansville, Indiana, J. E. Bailey, of Nashville, Tennessee, Henry M. Butler, of St. Louis, N. L. Glover, of Akron, Ohio, N. Coe Stewart, of Cleveland, and Orlando Blackman, of Chicago. These men were all pioneers, were all singing-school teachers, and they laid the foundations of school-music in their respective fields. Milton Z. Tinker taught for fifty years at Evansville, and J. E. Bailey nearly as long at Nashville. Nathan L. Glover and N. Coe Stewart both compiled school music books, and were both active in the Music Teachers National Association and the Music Section of the N. E. A. Mr. Glover organized the Ohio Music Teachers Association in 1878. The two men were intimately associated in their musical interests. Mr. Stewart conducted a six weeks' normal institute at Painesville, Ohio, in 1870, which Mr. Glover attended as a student. In 1871 Mr. Stewart conducted an institute at Akron, in which Mr. Glover acted as assistant teacher. N. Coe Stewart was widely known through his institute activities, which led to his appointment as supervisor of music in the schools of Cleveland and Akron in 1870. He soon was obliged to give his whole time to Cleveland, and in 1872 Mr. Glover took charge of the music at Akron, and held this position for 49 years, retiring in 1921. In 1918 The Nathan L. Glover School was named for him in recognition of his long and efficient service. N. Coe Stewart was one of the first to place the teaching of music in the hands of the grade teachers and to give them the necessary instruction in methods. He visited each class, held teachers' meetings every Saturday, and then made them responsible for their own class teaching. Others like Benjamin Jepson and George B. Loomis also worked through the grade teachers, but real supervision of music lessons was rare in this period. The modern practice in this respect came about slowly. For the most part the grade teachers did not feel it part of their duties to give music lessons, and this remained the general attitude toward music until the normal schools began to include that subject in the curriculum, and it was persuasively shown by an increasing number of supervisors that music could be taught one step at a time, like other subjects.

The work of Charles Aiken, of Cincinnati was mentioned in the preceding chapter. His son, Walter H. Aiken began teaching music in Middletown, Ohio, in 1874. He became supervisor of music at Hamilton, Ohio, in 1876. In 1879 he began teaching in the Cincinnati schools under Charles Aiken and his successor, G. F. Junkelmann. In 1900 he was appointed superintendent of music of the Cincinnati schools, in which position he has maintained the standards set by his father, besides being a leader in the school-music progress of the last quarter-century. His record of 54 years' continuous service is the longest in the history of public school music. Charles Aiken commenced his work in Cincinnati in 1842. Thus the work of father and son extends through a period of 86 years, lacking only four years of covering the entire history of music in the public schools.

Walter H. Aiken's life has been rich in labor and achievement. Besides handling the ordinary routine of music supervisor of a large city, he has been a brilliant chorus director, has edited some 2000 pages of *The Willis Collection of School Songs*, 200 of which he has orchestrated, and has trained hundreds of teachers at the University of Cincinnati. The important part taken by the school children in the Cincinnati Biennial Festivals is nationally known.

Besides being a musician Mr. Aiken is a nature lover and a trained botanist. He served for five years with the Cincinnati Natural History Society, and twenty-five years with the Lloyd Library in charge of a herbarium of some forty thousand plants.

In 1925 The Cincinnati Conservatory of Music conferred upon him the honorary degree of Doctor of Pedagogy. On this occasion Superintendent Randall J. Condon paid him the following tribute:— "Worthy son of a noble father: learned in science and in art; a lover of children, of birds and flowers and of all the gentle things in life; writer and teacher of music; a director of teachers and a leader of a great city. He has been true to the teachings of the past and has pioneered the way for the future. At home and abroad he is recognized as a sane and reliable exponent of the best thought and finest ideals in teaching music in the public schools, both vocal and instrumental, and in applying that teaching to the enrichment of community life."

In a previous chapter mention was made of the fact that Luther Whiting Mason was teaching in the Louisville Schools in 1852. He was born at Turner, Maine, in 1828, and spent his entire life in public school music work. This gave him the public school rather than the singing-school point of view. His work in Louisville attracted the favorable attention of members of the Germania Orchestra, then touring the country, and who visited his classes.

The following letter expresses their critical opinion of his teaching, and contains some details as to his method.

"We have been astonished at the success you have met with in regard to instructing pupils thoroughly and in so short a period, and do with pleasure acknowledge that we consider your mode the most practicable ever experienced. You have succeeded in a few months to make the pupils sing the scale in all intervals, such as thirds, fourths, fifths, etc., without their hesitating one moment, and have succeeded in making them thoroughly acquainted with the rudiments of music, without stuffing their heads with far-sought, and to the children, incomprehensible expressions."

"We are also pleased with their remarkable ability to write down any sound or note of the scale, such as you sing them, and their bold outpourings of their little voices, not showing any fear of uncertainty in soloing their exercises."

"Closing our remarks on this matter, we would add, that if vocal music were to be taught like this all over the States, we should hear less faulty singing and piano playing, such as amateurs, without any good basis of the art, are usually tormenting our ears with."

"Accept our wishes for your welfare and success, and believe us to be your most obedient servants."

This letter was signed by Carl Bergmann, Alfred Jaell, Carl Zerrahn, C. Plagman and Henry Band.[1]

In 1857 Mr. Mason left Louisville and began teaching in the schools of Cincinnati. Here he became acquainted with the school-music books of Christian Heinrich Hohmann, which were based upon the teaching of Johann Georg Nageli, an associate of Pestalozzi in the schools of Switzerland and Germany. He gave them a thorough study and persuaded Oliver Ditson to publish an English translation of the fifth edition in 1859. This publication was probably the first departure in this country from the type of Juvenile Song Books, compiled by Lowell Mason and others for use rather indiscriminatingly in singing-schools, public schools and Sunday Schools.

In 1864 Luther Whiting Mason was called to Boston to organize primary music instruction. This established a new precedent, for with the exception of perhaps Cincinnati, all music instruction in the public schools at this time was confined to the grammar grades and high school. With primary music instruction as an established fact, there was pressing need of music books planned to proceed progressively through all the grades. This need was supplied in 1870 by *The National Music Course*, compiled by Mr. Mason and published by Edwin Ginn the founder

[1]*Proceedings of Music Teachers National Association,* 1922, page 161.

of the publishing house of Ginn and Company.   The title of the books proved prophetic, for their use became practically universal.   A generation of school children became as familiar with their contents as a previous one had been with the Webster speller. Luther Whiting Mason may be considered the founder of school music methodology, for the *National Music Course* was not only the first completely planned course to receive national recognition—it was also the prototype of all the many methods which followed it.   Moreover, its influence was international, as a translation of this course was published in Leipsic, and used in German schools, and the method was adopted by the Japanese government for use in the schools of that country, following a three years' sojourn there by Mr. Mason as governmental music supervisor.

Mason's main contribution to music methods was in formulating instruction in the primary grades, more especially his philosophy of the approach to music reading, about which question, it may be said in passing, most of the differences of opinion among music specialists have arisen.

The song material of the *National Music Course* was largely German,—the same songs which we find today in numberless collections of German folk songs. Mason's philosophy of the approach to music reading was an application of that of James Currie, of Scotland, of which the following is quoted from one of

Page from Luther Whiting Mason's *First Music Reader*,
Ginn Brothers, 1874.
(By permission of Ginn and Company.)

Mason's books. "The proper view to take of a child learning to read is, that he is learning to recognize in printed or written forms, the words with which he is already familiar in speech. We only surround him with difficulties if we regard his reading book at this period as the means of extending his vocabulary." He applied this view of language reading to music teaching and thus became the first advocate of the song method.

He made use of the Tonic Sol-fa modulator and the Galin-Paris-Cheve notation, (a modified Tonic Sol-fa notation, but using numbers instead of syllables) the latter as a temporary step preceding the study of the staff. To enhance the feeling of measure rhythms he used the time names of the Galin system, though he advocated beating time with the hand to secure a firm feeling for the regular beat. It is interesting to note, in this connection, the profound influence upon American school music, not only of Pestalozzian pedagogy, but of the Tonic Sol-fa system.

Tonic Sol-fa began to be used in England about 1840.   Started by Elizabeth Glover, it was perfected by John Curwen, and became the accepted method of primary music education in the British schools. The basic principle of the system is the revival of the ancient movable DO, which the fixed DO, favored by the growing prevalence of instrumental study, had tended to displace.   The system teaches the tone relations of the scale from a vertical modulator, or tone ladder, following this with the notation, which is that of the initial letters of the so-fa syllables, printed horizontally, using no staff, but separating the measures by bars, the time divisions being indicated by the lineal distance between the syllables, and by an ingenious system of commas, dots and dashes.

During the generation of Mr. Mason and his contemporaries repeated attempts were made to introduce the Tonic Sol-fa notation in the schools of this country, and in fact it was used for a time in a

few places.   But our teachers balked at having to
teach two notations, having determined at any cost
to teach the staff.   They accepted and used, con-
sciously or unconsciously much of the Tonic Sol-fa
teaching of tone relations, and if it could have been
shown that time could be saved by teaching both the
Tonic Sol-fa and the staff notation, or that by this
process the latter could be better taught, perhaps
the attempt to introduce the Tonic Sol-fa system
might have succeeded.

In Mr. Mason's second book, for intermediate
grades, music reading was developed through a study
of the scale, first the scale of C, in which key were
studied the most common intervals, the problems of
the two even tones to the beat, the dotted quarter and
eighth, and also two-part singing, all in the key of
C.   Then followed in traditional order a study of
the other keys.   Referring to this long use of the Key
of C, Mr. Mason wrote, "I do not sympathize with
those who entertain so much anxiety about becoming
too familiar with the key of C.   There are other
difficulties than those of tone to be encountered and
overcome.   After the pupils have mastered the scale
so as to read readily in the key of C, let them in that
key wrestle with some of the hard things in time . . . .
I find no difficulty with children nine years of age, in
changing the places as to the pitch of the scale . . . .

All the difficulties that have been overcome in one key, as to tune and time, are under our feet forever in all the others."

Mason's philosophy of the approach to reading, now so familiar in the teaching of the primary grades, was decidedly novel to a generation teaching reading by the alphabet method, and the analogy between language and music, though acknowledged as a fact, was then considered too fanciful to be readily applied to music reading.   Nevertheless, the simple method outlined by Mason was widely if not expertly used, and the songs were learned and sung with pleasure by the children both at school and at home for many years.

The method of the *National Music Course* was the result of a wide acquaintance on the part of the author with the methods of teaching in the European schools, not only of music but other subjects as well, coupled with a keen sense of the need of American public schools.   In basing the beginnings of reading upon the rote song he broke entirely away from the traditional methods of the singing-schools, and was far in advance of his generation, but his treatment of the transposition of the scale and insistence on beating time with the hand followed the customary procedure of that institution, although with necessary adaptions to the immaturity of children.

The main difficulty with school-music in the period we are considering was essentially the same as today, a lack of knowledge of music on the part of many of the grade teachers, though the common stock of such knowledge has been undoubtedly growing year by year. But in the two decades following the Civil War the relation of the grade teacher to music teaching was by no means clear. Many felt that they should not be asked to teach music, and that it was an act of grace on their part to do so. They shared the rather common feeling that this was the business of the special music teachers. Hence the difficulty of successfully putting into operation over the entire country any method of teaching music, however admirable. On the other hand, in many places large and small excellent results were secured through the co-operation of the grade teachers.

In some reminiscences of public school music in this generation H. S. Perkins touches upon the uncertain status of the subject and the attitude of some teachers:—"In those earlier times thorough instruction in sight singing and the fundamentals, as taught in the other branches was not popular. Therefore rote singing occupied a large part of the lesson hour. Singing was looked upon as a recreation from other studies. Hence the teacher must be politic, and introduce pleasing songs with pretty stories. The young children must be tickled, all of the children must be entertained. A semi-annual or annual exhibition of the songs, and an occasional cantata must be given either in the school room or in a large hall to demonstrate to the parents, the public and the school board what the pupils could do in this specialty. The question did not come up—can the pupils read and sing simple music at sight? Have they learned the A, B, C's of music? The music lesson hour was not infrequently seized upon by the regular teachers to leave the room for a social visit in some other room. This left a roomful of "incorrigibles" in charge of the music teacher who had no authority to discipline the unruly; therefore he must resort to sweetmeats, flattery and tact to keep the pupils busy—to preserve order and to prevent a first class pandemonium. The prospective exhibitions helped to keep the children interested. To assemble one thousand children in a large hall, as I did several times, notably in Springfield, Massachusetts in 1865, for a public demonstration of the songs sung in unison and two parts, was the best chord the teacher could play. These efforts received the commendation of the parents, the people, the press and the school management."[1]

Herbert Griggs, a well known supervisor of music wrote thus of one of his boyhood music teachers;—"How easily I can recall our first music master coming into the room with his fiddle box under his arm. How anxiously I watched his every movement hoping to see him lay it on my desk and open it. When he would take out his bow, tighten up the

[1]*School Music*—May, 1908.

hairs and resin it, take out the fiddle, pick the strings and tune it, I would think what a wonderful man he was.   How tickled I was when he broke a string. That was the joy of it."

"But when he pointed his bow at me; told me to 'stand, sir,' and asked 'what are those two flats for, sir,' or 'if a whole note has four beats in 4-4 time how many beats will a dotted eighth have in 3-2 time,' or when he would stand me on the floor for trying to sing bass like the big boys, (I was about ten years of age), or rap me on the head with his bow for not singing louder, that was the sorrow of it.   How he used to stamp his foot, wiggle his head, scrape that fiddle, and count and sing, sing and count.   Such was the style of teaching music in the public schools years ago."[1]

On the other hand, William Lyon Phelps, of Yale University, speaks of his school-music teacher as follows;—"I studied music under Benjamin Jepson when I was five years old.   He taught music to the children of New Haven for fifty years and was always brilliant, persuasive and charming.   New Haven owes an unpayable debt to him and his memory will always be held in high esteem.   It is my belief that children in the public schools should be taught to read music as he taught it to us."[2]

The giving of annual exhibitions already alluded

[1] *N. E. A. Proceedings, Music Section,* 1890.
[2] *M. T. N. A. Proceedings,* 1922—paper by Ralph Baldwin, page 166.

to of large choruses of children in an auditorium or
on patriotic occasions massed in the public square
has always been accepted as a peculiarly fitting and
appropriate function of the public schools. The
first such concert in Boston seems to have been in
1858 when 1200 children sang in Music Hall under
the direction of Carl Zerrahn, who then had charge
of music in the Normal School. These exhibitions
were given annually thereafter in Boston, and they
may have helped to establish the general custom
throughout the country. Frequently these occasions
took the form of pageants or flower festivals such as
The Coronation of the Rose, and the *Festival of the
Rose.* The war songs of George F. Root, and such
selections as the *Anvil Chorus, Angels Ever Bright
and Fair, Hail the Conquering Hero Comes,* and of
course *My Country 'Tis of Thee* and *The Star
Spangled Banner* were much used.

Summing up the period immediately following
the Civil War, we may say that music took its place
by general acceptance in the public schools, and that
systematic, graded work from the first grade to the
high school began in this period. Lowell Mason
died in 1872. The Boston Academy of Music had
ceased operations in 1848. The influence of the
musical conventions, which continued for several decades to carry on the Academy's pedagogic aims and
purposes, in turn became deflected into other channels, and ceased to affect public school music. From

now on school-music teaching became a distinct profession, absorbed in its relation, not to the general field of music, with which until the present century it largely lost touch, but rather to the field of general education, and in particular to the problem of teaching music to all the children of all the people.   The need of graded material and a well organized method was filled by the *National Music Course*.

School-music teachers, facing the conditions implicit in having to teach music to every child, gradually evolved routines and techniques of teaching which were neither those of the singing-school nor of the private teacher.   And with this evolution arose varying conceptions of how and what children should be taught.   These conceptions grew up naturally from working with children.   Two especially may be mentioned—one, that the pupils should be taught as many songs as possible with the help of the teacher, a sort of rote-note process, the other that they should learn to read music in order to sing the songs.

FIRST WEAVER SUMMER SCHOOL. WESTFIELD. MASS.. 1900.

HOSEA EDSON HOLT

FRANCIS E. HOWARD

SAMUEL WINKLEY COLE

JULIA ETTIE CRANE

STERRIE A. WEAVER

FREDERICK H. RIPLEY

Chapter V

CONCENTRATING UPON MUSIC READING
(1885-1905)

MUSIC won its first introduction into the public schools in 1838 largely upon the proof that all children could learn to sing. During the next forty years, all through its introductory period and while it was gradually crystallizing into a school subject, it was almost wholly in the hands of the special music teacher, who gave practically all of the instruction. After the Civil War grade teachers here and there began to teach music, but it was not until the twenty-five year interval beginning about 1885 that the subject was placed squarely in the hands of the grade teacher. This was a momentous change for school-music, and it inevitably forced attention upon the teaching of music reading, which had in the past been wholly the problem of the special teacher. Music became in fact as well as in name a school subject, and how to teach music reading became the paramount question of the age. It was in fact the first problem which school-music set itself seriously to solve.

The era was one of tremendous geographical expansion of school-music, of large consequent demand for music material, resulting in the publishing of many courses of music books, of establishing summer institutes for training music teachers, and of forming professional school-music associations.

In the three-year interval between 1886 and 1889, as shown by official reports there was a gain of 33 percent in the number of places employing special music teachers. If we assume this as roughly the average rate of increase thereafter it will account for the practically universal teaching of music in the schools at the present time. During the period we are considering the number of introductions more than quadrupled.

The word which best expresses the inner spirit of this period is efficiency. The titanic growth of industry after the Civil War profoundly affected American life. Big business put the stamp of efficiency not only upon our industrial and economic life, but it brought its challenge into the public schools. The efficient teacher, skilled in the methods of Herbart, and the master of the technique of the recitation became the desideratum of every school superintendent.

The elementary school began to undergo a profound change in the expansion of the curriculum, in promoting efficiency by flexible grading, and in various forms of reorganization. The grade teacher became expert in handling a large number of studies with constantly improving methods. Music began to compete for time and attention with this increasingly complicated program. The old half-hour music period occupied by the special music teacher was a thing of the past. The regular teacher was expected to teach music along with the other subjects and in an average period of fifteen minutes. Under these conditions school-music had to take account of stock. Music had now to prove, not its value as an art, or as contributing to our common life, but that it was a subject which could be taught efficiently by the grade teacher.

The old source of supply for trained music teachers, namely, the singing-school and convention, was by this time dried up, especially in the East. The private teacher had displaced the singing-school teacher. The normal schools had not begun to train music supervisors, with the notable exception of the Potsdam Musical Institute, which Julia Ettie Crane opened in 1884. Superintendents were forced to take persons untrained in pedagogy, relying entirely upon their musicianship, supplemented by common sense. Music was being introduced too rapidly to secure invariably even trained musicians as teachers. The country no longer consisted of the land east of the Mississippi. The transcontinental railway had doubled our commonwealths almost overnight.

The *National Music Books* had now been in use

for fourteen years. Their pedagogy and song material, especially the latter, were familiar to all
music teachers. In due time this very familiarity
brought about a reaction. There was a growing dis-
trust of the rote song approach to music reading,
and song singing itself became an object of suspicion
as being merely entertaining without helping directly
to a mastery of the printed page. The music supervisor had had little guide except the printed suggestions in the music books, supplemented by his own
pedagogical ability. He thus became more or less
a law into himself, a condition highly favorable for
developing individual initiative, and out of which
grew a characteristic feature of the period, namely,
the editing and publishing of a large number of
school-music readers.

Of those who evolved a new method one of the
first as well as one of the most influential men of the
period was Hosea Edson Holt, of Boston. He was
born in Ashburnham, Massachusetts, February 20,
1836, worked on a farm as a boy and then learned
the turner's trade. During the day time he worked
at his trade and at night taught singing-schools.
He served in the Civil War as a bandsman and then
decided to make music his profession. After studying with Benjamin F. Baker and John W. Tufts in
Boston, he taught music at Wheaton Seminary and
the Bridgewater Normal School. It was here that
his success as a music pedagogue began to attract

wide attention. From 1869 until his death in 1898 he was one of the music supervisors of the Boston schools. He made a strong impress upon his generation, not only upon his fellow music teachers, but upon school superintendents and general educators. He was a skillful teacher, a forceful thinker and a brilliant speaker. In the unhampered field afforded by the Boston schools, he worked out a new plan of music instruction for all the elementary grades. This plan was so distinctively his own that it became known as the Holt method.

His associate in this enterprise was John W. Tufts, his former teacher, and a highly gifted musician, who edited and composed the music for the various books required, which collectively were called *The Normal Music Course.*

John Wheeler Tufts was born at Dover, New Hampshire, in 1825. From 1846 to 1848 he studied at Leipsic with Mocheles and Hauptman. Returning to this country he was active as organist and conductor in Bangor and Portland, Maine. In 1880 he settled in Boston, was appointed organist of King's Chapel, and became prominent as a teacher and oratorio coach. He was a man of wide culture, with other interests than those of music, especially in the field of physical science, and was a member of the Boston Scientific Society. He had also a decided talent for drawing, which he turned to good account in the preparation of his music books, in which he was the first to use pictures illustrative of the text, and drawn by himself.

Tuft's association with Holt quickened into life a plan he had long been contemplating of writing a music course for schools in order to provide material which could be used by the grade teacher.   It had been the custom in most places for the music teacher to visit each school at weekly or fortnightly intervals, and in the meantime no regular music work was done. The books were thus intended to serve a double purpose, first, to offer plenty of well graded exercises and songs in such form that the grade teacher could conduct the music lesson successfully, and second, to cover every problem so thoroughly that the children would be compelled to become music readers. This step-wise plan was carried out with relentless logic.   Every tonal and rhythmic difficulty had its orderly place and its illustrative exercise.   The music was written contrapuntally, the harmonic element in the two and three-part music being the result of two and three melodies written one below another—a wide departure from the *National Music Course*, which was frankly harmonic, with its prevailing thirds and sixths in the texture of the two-part songs.

The method itself was based on mastery of the major scale, taught as a melody, and from which were developed all the intervals. . Much use was made of modulator, charts and the five fingers of the hand to represent the staff when dictating tones. Beating time with the hand was definitely abandoned. The feeling for time was regarded as not muscular but mental, and was to be gained by watching a swinging pendulum, while repeating the Galin-Paris-Cheve time language. Much emphasis was laid upon dictation, both tonal and rhythmic.

The *Normal Music Course* consisted of First, Second and Third Readers for the elementary grades and *The Euterpean Song Book* for high schools. There were also charts paralleling the elementary books to be used for class drill on tone and rhythm.

The definiteness of the method re-enforced by Mr. Holt's unbounded faith and enthusiasm and his great power as a teacher, gained from the start many adherents who visited his classes in the Boston schools. The books were published by D. Appleton and Company in 1883, but in 1885 the publishing rights were secured by Silver, Burdett and Company who started their publishing business with the *Normal Music Course* and the *Ward Rational Method of Reading*. It was not long before the *Normal* books were extensively used in every part of the country, including places where music was being introduced for the first time.

A method, however, will not teach itself; it must be demonstrated. Therefore in 1884 Mr. Holt opened a summer school at Lexington, Massachusetts, which attracted students from many states, including beginners and experienced supervisors. This was the first school to be organized exclusively for the training of music supervisors. It did much to enhance the vogue of the *Normal Music Course*, and to increase among its students a realization of school-

NORMAL MUSIC COURSE.

FIRST READER.

Part I.

EXERCISES FOR STUDY AND PRACTICE.

Page from *The Normal Music Course, First Reader,* New and Revised Edition, by Tufts and Holt, 1892.
(By permission of Silver, Burdett and Company, publishers.)

music as a profession, with its own special problems, distinct from those of the singing-school on the one hand, and of the private teacher on the other. Here was created the enthusiasm for the teaching technique of the new method, which carried it far and wide over the country and gave it a leading place in school-music for a generation.

The *Normal Music Course* in due time was followed by others. For several years it shared the field with Luther Whiting Mason's revision of the *National Music Course*, published in 1885 by Ginn and Company as the *New National Music Course*. In 1892, Silver, Burdett and Company published *The Cecilian Series of Study and Song*, written by John W. Tufts. The same year King, Richardson and Company published *The American Music System*, a series of school music books compiled by Friedrich Zuchtmann, of Springfield, Massachusetts. The chief contribution of this series was the stress given to the treatment of children's voices.

In 1895, The John Church Company published the *Model Music Course*, edited by John A. Broekhoven and A. J. Gantvoort of Cincinnati. This course consisted of a book for each grade, with chapter divisions arranged in four lessons, each covering a week's work. The same year, 1895, the *Natural Course in Music* was published by The American Book Company. The editors were Frederick H. Ripley, head master of one of the Boston

schools, and Thomas Tapper, the well known authority on music pedagogy.   This was a strong course,
with several distinctive features, all directed toward
simplification of method for the teacher and learning
for the pupil.

The ten year vogue of the *Normal Music Course*
had gradually revealed the disturbing fact that
though the children mastered the tonal and rhythmic
problems by means of its elaborate drills, they could
not combine them so as to read music readily.   The
authors of the *Natural Music Course* attempted to
avoid this weakness by a simplified procedure.   In
a paper read before the Music Teachers National
Association in 1917 Mr. Ripley explained how the
course came to be prepared and its pedagogy.   The
following paragraphs from this paper cover the main
points.

"In 1877, Mr. Julius Eichberg, then Director
of Public School Music Instruction in Boston, asked
me to consider the presentation of music in the public
schools from the standpoint of the grade teacher,
to whom music teaching was a mere item in a great
body of school work, and to present for his consideration the results of my efforts.   I gladly undertook
the work.   I began by making a study of the then
current theories and practices in the public schools.
I collected all of the so-called systems for study, and
I became a constant inquirer at the doors of our
famous music supervisors."

"My problem, not at first apprehended, but gradually perceived, was to eliminate the so-called theory of music (now frequently spoken of as technical teaching) and to treat music symbols as the representation of known tone relations, pure and simple, without why and wherefore. It was necessary, then, to emancipate the grade teachers from the definitions with which they were struggling."

"This idea came to me as a result of observing Mr. H. E. Holt's work. Mr. Holt declared that relative tonality should be made a perfectly definite, almost concrete thing, in the mind of the pupil, and that music notation should express this relation as an absolute and unexplained symbol, just as the teacher of literary reading presents the symbols of ideas, without explaining the spelling, the punctuation, and the arrangement of order in which the words are placed."

"The idea was fundamental and served to modify the music work very materially. But in the attempt to develop the perception of tone relation, artificial devices were so extensively used that the effort resulted in but small advance in the pupil's power to read music. While he could respond rapidly and accurately to number dictation, as sing three, sing five and the like, and hand signs, finger staves, and ladders were all very familiar, the interpretation of the melody when expressed upon the staff was slow and imperfect."

"After a protracted study of these ideas and much practice in the use of them in school, I concluded that the one vital idea was contained in Mr. Holt's repeated assertion that real musicianship was based on the perception of tone relations as a perfectly definite thing.   All the rest went by the board. Having reached this conclusion I set myself the task of devising a presentation of music which should be entirely free of technicalities, so called, but which should make the notation as it now exists an actual, vital expression of a real thing to all pupils who beheld it.   Definition and theory were entirely eliminated.   Number, hand signs, ladders and the like were omitted.   Rhythm was joined to melody, and the interval as a study disappeared from elementary work.   All representations were musical and complete."

"I have already mentioned the fact that when I began to think about these matters various forms of time language were being extensively used in the schools.   I mastered these very fully, and gave them complete and extended trials.   I found an almost impassable gulf between the practice in time language and its application to the notation as it appeared on the staff.   This obstacle was perceived by others, and the practice sprang up of making several trips over the music as a preliminary to singing.   Thus, first, the tones were made out either by number, or by syllable, and then the rhythm by means of time language was given in monotone. Finally an attempt was made to render the tones and the rhythms together, in other words, to sing the melody at sight—though evidently not at first sight."

"In meeting this difficulty I clung still to my idea of having nothing unmusical enter into the presentation. I accidentally hit upon the scheme which I found out afterwards was common in France, namely, the rhythm-building scheme. That is, a certain note is adopted as a standard, this note is tied with other notes so as to produce all higher note values used in the exercise. Thus in four-four meter, taking the quarter note as the standard, two quarters tied give the half, three quarters tied give the dotted half, and four quarters tied give the whole note. Thus the child, beating quarters, passes easily from the representation in tied quarters to the presentation in notes of higher values, and also the use of the dot. Proceeding in the same way, but taking the eighth note as a standard, everything above the eighth in value is worked out."[1]

The *Natural Course in Music* made an important contribution to school-music pedagogy, and was long and extensively used in many sections of the country. The same philosophy and general method was incorporated some years later in two other music courses, the *Melodic* and *Harmonic Courses* respectively, edited by the same authors.

[1]Frederick H. Ripley—*How to Promote Musical Appreciation Without Technical Work*—*M. T. N. A. Proceedings*, 1917.

In 1899, Francis E. Howard of Bridgeport, Connecticut, compiled the *Novello Music Course*, which was published by The H. W. Gray Company. Mr. Howard is best known to music supervisors and voice teachers as the author of *The Child Voice in Singing*. He was an expert in children's voices, and through addresses and demonstrations given with children at conventions of teachers he helped to spread a knowledge of the child voice and the importance of its right use. His other main contribution to school-music pedagogy was his emphasis upon learning to do by doing. He believed that nothing should come between the child and the music he is trying to read. He did not believe in elaborate preparation for reading by means of various drill exercises. To him, real music reading did not consist merely in singing one note after another. The meaning came through the onward rhythmic flow of the music itself. This view of music reading pedagogy, which was shared by other supervisors, came rather late in the period. It was a natural reaction from the many methods which had been published and was an attempt to reduce the whole matter to its lowest terms.

By this time the prevailing method of teaching sight reading, the scale-drill method, had been on trial for fifteen years with widely varying results. In spite of the fact that the purpose of it all was to develop skill in music reading, the general practice in the school room tended to emphasize knowledge rather than skill. Many children learned to read music, to be sure, just as they had done in previous epochs, and we now know that this ability came from the amount of actual reading they did, which was, of course, considerable.

Some of the leading music supervisors were famous for their skill in leading classes through elaborate scale work or various forms of rhythm drill, an example which was more or less successfully imitated by the rank and file of their followers. Speaking of this general practice, T. L. Roberts writes;—"The major part of the music period was then spent in singing from modulators, through the medium of a pointer in the hand of the teacher. There were exceptions to this rule, but I speak of the general situation. Classes were then expert in singing tones of the scale thus pointed out, and, after having had this modulator training for years they would sing correctly the most difficult of intervals, for the different tones of the major scale, as 'relative mental objects,' were as well known in the mind through the ear as material objects are through the eye. Some wonderful exhibitions of proficiency were given before institutes and conventions. But alas, the ability of children to read fluently and rapidly written music containing these intervals or even much simpler ones, was sadly lacking. Why? Simply from lack of practice in reading music written in the ordinary way. The mistake was made in treating it as not simply a step, but almost the entire platform."[1]

There stands out with striking distinctness from among his contemporaries of this epoch the figure of Sterrie A. Weaver, of Westfield, Massachusetts. Like the prophet Elijah of old, he suddenly appeared on the scene of school-music, delivered his message, completed his work, and as suddenly departed. His character was strong, self reliant and ruggedly honest. His personality was simple, and vibrant with energy and deep feeling. His intellect was keen and penetrating, and he was a born teacher. It was his mission to evolve a method of teaching sight reading which was devoid of all the paraphernalia of the period, and to prove that every child can be taught to read music.

Sterrie A. Weaver was born in New London, Connecticut, March 16, 1853. When he was eight years old, the family moved to New Hartford, Connecticut, where he grew to manhood. He went to evening singing-schools, studied at the New England Conservatory and in Germany, and began supervising at Torrington, Connecticut, adding the towns of Westfield and Amherst. To this triple job he added the directorship of music at the Westfield Normal School, and in 1900 became editor of the

[1]*School Music,* May, 1908.

school-music department of *The Musical Courier*.
In 1900 he opened a summer school for supervisors
of music at Westfield. In 1903 he took an eighth
grade class from the Torrington Schools to the meeting of the music section of the N. E. A. at Jordan
Hall, Boston, where he demonstrated before a large
audience the ability of his pupils to read music by
any test. He died in 1904, just as his work was
becoming nationally known. His influence upon
school music was healthy and invigorating; he
applied scientific methods to the problem of music
reading, and he tirelessly urged the supervisors of
the country, through his summer school, public addresses and written articles to take a scientific attitude toward their work.

His only working tools for teaching were the
blackboard, his own voice and those of the children.
He discarded pointers, ladders, modulators and hand
signs. Even music books were unnecessary except
as a test of the ability of the children to sing at sight.
He aimed to be able to hand a child a piece of music
and have him sing it without help. Such skill de-
manded a tonal and rhythmic vocabulary every detail
of which the pupil must be ready to use. Eye and
ear must be perfectly co-ordinated. Each tone of
the vocabulary was taught by imitation and related
to all the other tones. The singing was done by the
entire class or by individuals as called for. The
pitch of the key tone was constantly shifted to keep

the ear alert.   The ear training was immediately
followed by eye training, the teacher writing exercises on the board, and frequently changing the staff
position of DO.   The rhythmic details were learned
in the same way by imitation.   One, two, three and
four beat sounds and the fractional divisions were
taught separately and combined visually with those
already learned and with the tonal vocabulary.   All
time difficulties were reduced to a single beat unit,
using a total of seven "time motions."   The blackboard exercises began and ended with any tone or
any kind of note, thus keeping the tonal and rhythmic
brain responsive to every demand of the printed
music.   The teacher never pointed to the notes, nor
did she beat the time.   She wrote the exercise,
stepped back from the board, sounded DO, said
'Sing', and the class sang, keeping their own time.
Such results meant the ruthless cutting out of most
of the cumbersome devices which had grown up during the period.   The governing principles of this
procedure were not new, but their combined application to teaching reading was a new contribution to
school music pedagogy.

The keystone of the Weaver method was the
individual singing child.   His plan was flexible
enough to meet the varying abilities of children in
the same class, and was self-regulating.   In this
respect Mr. Weaver may be called our first exponent
of tests and measurements in sight reading, and this

stands out as his main contribution to school-music, and, in the writer's opinion the main contribution of the period. The spirit of this epoch has been mentioned as that of efficiency. Sterrie A. Weaver was the embodiment of that spirit.

At about the same time that Mr. Weaver was working out the reading problem Thaddeus P. Giddings was doing the same thing successfully in Illinois, though by a different method. Mr. Giddings' public school career began with a varied experience as music teacher in his home town of Anoka, Minnesota, and in a number of rural schools, and also at Moline, Illinois. From there he went to Oak Park, Illinois, where his methods of teaching music reading became widely known. In 1912 he became director of music of the schools of Minneapolis.

Mr. Weaver used books sparingly in his work; his results came through the use of the blackboard and individual singing slips. Mr. Giddings' philosophy is more nearly that of Francis E. Howard, namely, learning to read by reading, not from the blackboard but from the book. His children read page after page and book after book keeping their own time by tapping the beat, much of this being done individually. His motto may be summed up as "Hands off—let the children do their own learning." By this method the children acquire skill in reading and they read many books. Regarding this point Mr. Giddings writes in a personal letter;—

"Whatever success I may have had is largely due to the free and unrestricted use of plenty of material. There are now in the Minneapolis course of study in music for the eight grades twenty-one books that all MUST sing through. There are eight more they may sing through. Many of the schools sing them all. There are in the high schools twenty-six sets of books that all may sing through if they are smart enough. With all this material at hand it would be wonderful if the pupils could not read music and like it."

Benjamin Jepson, of New Haven, Connecticut, who began his work in 1865, continued in active service throughout this entire period and well into the next. Seventy-five percent of his pupils could read music. "Solo singing" was a feature of his method, and he was one of the first to have systematic individual singing.

Thus by devious routes and a variety of methods the problem of music reading was worked out in this epoch. The outstanding successes were made by those who discovered the necessity of individual work and of keeping the issue clear of non essentials.

Professional study of school-music, however, was by no means confined to the school room. The publishers of the leading music courses followed the example of Mr. Holt and conducted summer schools for the training of teachers, thus rendering an indispensable service, at a time when the normal schools were not generally prepared to give such training. At these summer schools the leading music supervisors of the country exemplified the methods advocated by each school. Not only were the methods thoroughly explained in detail, but valuable instruction was given in the handling of classes, in the art of song leading, and the treatment of children's voices. One of the most potent forces of the summer schools was the chorus singing. The combination of a good director, and a chorus of intelligent singers with well trained voices, together with the strong bond of a common professional interest produced an unusual and unforgettable quality of choral result. The single inspiration of the chorus sent hundreds of music teachers back to their work with a new realization of the power of choral singing, and a determination to have it in their own schools at any cost.

Though these schools were each devoted to teaching the pedagogy of a particular method, their general atmosphere was by no means commercial. Their educational level was high, and one may wonder how thousands of music teachers would have received adequate training without them.

One of the valuable features of the summer schools was the opportunity of meeting other music teachers from all parts of the land, and talking over their common interests. Not only were the various methods analyzed and teaching devices compared, but the values of educational theories were discussed and sifted, all of which tended toward a broader professional outlook. It was this feature of the summer schools which prepared the way for the marvelous development of organizations of music teachers in the twentieth century, and which have had such powerful reactions upon the progress of school-music.

The first summer school exclusively for school music training was held in 1884 at Lexington, Massachusetts, under Hosea E. Holt. Then in 1886 the National Summer School of Music was started in Boston with the following faculty;—Luther Whiting Mason, N. Lincoln, C. R. Bill, George A. Veazie, O. B. Brown, S. H. Hadley, J. B. Sharland, Henry G. Carey and Leonard B. Marshall. A western extension of this school was opened in Chicago in 1903. The National School was maintained by Ginn and Company.

In 1889, Silver, Burdett and Company started The American Institute of Normal Methods at Lake Geneva, Wisconsin, with H. E. Holt as director. In 1892 the Eastern session of the American Institute was incorporated in Boston with H. E. Holt, John W. Tufts, Leonard B. Marshall and Samuel W. Cole as members of the faculty. During its early years Frederick A. Lyman of Syracuse, New York, was also one of the teachers. The American Institute was a continuation under another name of Mr. Holt's Lexington school already mentioned. Both the East-

SUMMER SCHOOL, LEXINGTON, MASSACHUSETTS, 1884.
ORGANIZED BY HOSEA E. HOLT.

PHILIP C. HAYDEN

WILLIAM L. TOMLINS

CHARLES H. CONGDON

HELEN PLACE MOSER

FRANCES E. CLARK

ALBERT G. MITCHELL

ern and the Western sessions of the Institute have been held annually to the present.

In the late nineties The American Book Company opened the New School of Methods in Chicago with Thomas Tapper as director. With him were associated prominent supervisors, including Walter Aiken and Hollis Dann. There were also a few year-round schools which offered training in school-music, such as the Thomas Normal Training School at Detroit, the outgrowth of summer sessions held for a few years beginning in 1892, and the Crosbie Adams School in Chicago.

Extensive and accurate data regarding the summer schools is difficult to obtain. It exists almost wholly in the fleeting memories of those who attended them. Valuable information of this kind was furnished the author by Osbourne McConathy in the following letter;—

"The first summer school which I attended was the Emma A. Thomas school in Detroit. As I recall it I attended this school in 1894, although I believe it was opened the year before. It is this school to which Mrs. Clark so recently referred in the meeting of the 'Pioneers.' Mrs. Thomas was the head of the school, and it was the outgrowth of this summer school which ultimately became the Thomas Normal Training School, which for so many years was conducted by Mrs. Thomas' daughter. The faculty of the school was led by Luther Whiting Mason, who had associated with him George A. Veazie, James McLaughlin, Mrs. Agnes C. Heath, Mrs. Thomas and others whose names I do not now recall. The school was held under the auspices of Ginn and Company, with Clarence C. Birchard as manager and E. W. Newton as assistant manager.

"At the close of this session in Detroit, I went to Boston where another summer school under the management of Ginn and Company was held in the old New England Conservatory on Franklin Square. Members of the Boston faculty under the leadership of Luther Whiting Mason were James McLaughlin, George A. Veazie, Frederick R. Chapman, the supervisor of music in Cambridge, Massachusetts, and Enos W. Pearson, supervisor of music at Nashua, New Hampshire.

"Upon the close of this session Mr. Mason and I went down to Maine where we held a summer session at Turner Center, a little spot made famous by its creamery. Turner Center is about nine or ten miles from the nearest railroad, and our object was to train teachers of country schools in music, physical education, drawing and reading. We had about sixty students who came from miles around to attend this session, and it was the outgrowth of the friendship which Mr. Mason and I formed during this summer and especially at the Turner Center school which grew into our intimacy and into the collaboration with Mr. Mason. This resulted in the *Mason Music*

Course published in 1896 by Ginn and Company and designed particularly for rural schools. The *Mason Music Course* was distinctive in that it had two text books and a manual for teachers which gave instructions and directions and included accompaniments to the songs of the text books.

"The following summer, as I recall it, in 1895, occurred the first school of The American Book Company with their new series, *The Natural Music Course* by Ripley and Tapper.

"The school of the American Book Company was held at Cataumet, on Cape Cod. Cataumet was the summering place of Mr. Ripley and the sessions of the school were held on his cottage front porch and in his living room. I recall very distinctly the sessions under Mr. Ripley and Mr. Tapper and social events in the evenings at the little hotel and in neighboring summer cottages.

"Just how long I remained in Cataumet I do not now recall though I believe I did not stay throughout the session. Instead I went to a summer school conducted by Ginn and Company at Plymouth, New Hampshire. Mr. Enos W. Pearson, who was later the supervisor of music in Philadelphia for so many years, was at that time connected with the Plymouth Normal School as well as filling the position of supervisor of the Nashua schools. The head of the faculty was James McLaughlin, and other teachers were George A. Veazie and Mr. Pearson. It was during this summer that the editorial board for the Educational Music Series was in session although Mr. Mason did not attend at summer school.   Mr. Newton was there and Mr. McLaughlin especially was very much occupied with his work on the course.

"Following my session at Plymouth I went again to Maine where Mr. Mason, Mr. Fred H. Butterfield (father of Walter) some other teachers and myself conducted two sessions for rural teachers, one in Buckfield and the other in Turner Center. The following year, 1896 was marked by the death of Luther Whiting Mason.

"During this summer Clarence Birchard conducted a summer school at Hingham, Massachusetts, under the auspices of the American Book Company. I had been in Buckfield with Mr. Mason and went from there to Hingham.   I recall the Hingham session very distinctly because Mr. Birchard had gathered a most exceptional faculty.   There were William L. Tomlins, Julia Ettie Crane, Francis E. Howard, Hollis Dann and others who together formed an unsual combination.   My stay at Hingham was cut short by the sudden death of Mr. Mason and I went back to Maine.   The school under Mr. Birchard's direction held a memorial service for Mason before I left.

"That summer Butterfield and I with several others conducted the summer school at Canton, Maine, which Mr. Mason had planned to handle.

This session was the last of the sessions for rural school teachers, an experiment which was decidedly interesting and I think productive of good.

"The following summer, 1897, I spent chiefly in Maine, though I recall that either in that summer or the one following, I visited a couple of times a session of a summer school conducted by Mr. Birchard and the American Book Company in Symphony Chambers, Boston.

"These are my recollections of my early summer school days. Much is vague in my memory although certain pictures stand out clearly in connection with each of the various schools I have mentioned."

The summer school opened by Sterrie A. Weaver in 1900 has already been mentioned. Upon Mr. Weaver's death in 1904 this school was taken over by Ralph L. Baldwin under whose able leadership it grew rapidly in numbers and prestige under the name Institute of Musical Pedagogy, with headquarters at Northampton, Massachusetts.

In 1884, Julia Ettie Crane started the Crane Normal Music Institute at Potsdam, New York, the first normal music school to be opened in the United States. Miss Crane had earlier been associated with William E. Sherwood and William Mason in some of the old normal institutes. She was a graduate of the Potsdam Normal State College, and was allowed by the State of New York to link up her school with this institution so as to give practical teaching to her pupils in the regular grades of the practice department. A special diploma was granted by the State to the graduates of the Crane Normal Institute.

Although Miss Crane was a normal school specialist, her professional activities brought her into close contact with supervisors of music and musicians from all sections of the country. The following sentences from an address delivered before the Music Teachers National Association in 1912 throw light upon the dubious standing of school-music among professional musicians in the early days;—"When your chairman suggested to me the subject of this paper, the history of the growth of public school music passed before my mind in a sort of panorama. I found myself back in the early days of my teaching, listening to a prophetic sense which told me that the school room needed music to give it its highest efficiency, and yet, finding that music as ordinarily taught in the public schools fell far short of the height which it might reach. I heard again the slighting remarks of professional musicians whenever the subject of school-music was broached. I heard the denunciation of voice teachers because of the quality of tone allowed in the public schools, and the prohibitions of choir masters that no member of their choir should be allowed to sing in school. I saw myself once more in attendance at State and National Teachers' Associations, where voice, piano, organ, and musical theory were given careful consideration, while school-music, if mentioned at all, was received with a contemptuous attitude which plainly indicated its standing in the musical world."

However deserved such a disparaging attitude may once have been, it is unquestionably true that during the last quarter of the nineteenth century were laid the foundations of the striking advance in school-music which has characterized the last twenty-five years. And that the results of the music work in the grades were of substantial and solid quality in the former period is attested by choral achievements which were directly related to elementary music work. As early as 1875 a chorus of over 300 graduates of the New Haven schools gave *The Creation, Messiah* and *Elijah* under Benjamin Jepson's direction. Fifteen years later, in 1890, Samuel W. Cole gave what was probably the first rendition of a complete oratorio with a high school chorus. This was a performance of *The Creation* at Dedham, Massachusetts, with orchestra and eminent soloists. In 1891 this was followed by a performance of *Messiah*. Two years later, in 1893, at Moline, Illinois, Thaddeus P. Giddings gave *The Creation* with a high school chorus of 150 voices, the entire membership of the school, the bass and soprano solos being taken by pupils, and the tenor solos by the director. A piano and organ supported the chorus, the piano being played by one of the pupils.

Such ambitious undertakings were of course unusual. They were pioneer work of a kind which became more and more frequent with each succeeding decade. But smaller choral works such as cantatas were successfully given by a large number of secondary schools. The high school music books of the period, edited by such men as Eichberg, Veazie and Tufts were of a high order of excellence, containing standard part songs and selections from operas and oratorios, and school-music publishers had already begun to issue well edited choruses in pamphlet form to supply a growing demand for supplementary music for both grammar and high schools.

SUMMARY

The period treated in this chapter began about 1885 and continued into the new century. During this epoch the old district school system largely disappeared. Supervisory control under the administration of a school superintendent, with supervising principals and supervisors of special branches became the rule, and the grade teacher took over the teaching of the daily music lesson. The special music teacher who formerly did all the teaching evolved into the music supervisor who directed the work of the grade teacher. To meet these changed conditions the *Normal* and other music courses were compiled and published. Success in school-music meant success in teaching music reading, and the best energy and thought of music teachers went into a study of this problem. Rote singing became largely taboo, and general song singing in the grades was given rather scant attention for its own sake. And yet in giving its main attention to a mastery of the printed page and proving that practically all children could be taught to read music the school-music profession raised the subject from a doubtful status to a secure place in the curriculum. It was a necessary and indispensable step in the evolution of school-music. The solution of the reading problem, the discovery of the child voice and the individual singing child were the three outstanding achievements of the period.

Chapter VI

THE TURN OF THE CENTURY

DURING the last decade of the nineteenth century the whole field of education was affected by two apparently contradictory but really complementary forces. One of these was the culmination of the influence of the Herbartian pedagogy, shown in enthusiasm for perfecting the method of the recitation, laying stress upon detailed plans, and emphasizing the instructional side of teaching. The other was the beginning of the child study movement, which emphasized spirit rather than method. One magnified the activities of the teacher, the other those of the child.

In the field of music these two forces were shown on the one hand by the perfecting of a teaching technique which proved that every child might be taught to read music, and on the other by a demand for more real music, more songs having beauty and charm, in the music lesson. The song idea soon became formulated as a method of teaching music reading, with song as the basis, and commonly known as the "song method." Exercises were still used in this method, but they were developed from the songs.

In using rote songs as a basis for primary music reading, this method had kinship with that of Luther Whiting Mason, the father of school music methodology.

A timely and long needed opportunity to bring these two points of view before the whole profession was now afforded by the beginning of school-music journalism. It is true that this need had been partially met by occasional articles in current musical magazines such as *The Musician* and *Music*, the latter edited by W. S. B. Mathews, and frankly critical in its attitude. Also in 1899 *The Musical Courier* had started a department for school music under the editorship of Sterrie A. Weaver. But it was not until 1900, just at the turn of the century that two periodicals devoted solely to school music interests made their first appearance. These were *School Music*, edited and published by Helen Place, then supervisor of music of Indianapolis, and *School Music Monthly*, edited and published by Philip C. Hayden, of Quincy, Illinois.

Miss Place's journal was intended to serve as an interpretive organ of the "new education" in the field of music. As stated in the first issue, its aims were to "keep its readers in touch with the best that is being done toward working out the teaching of this subject (music) on the basis of the new education." Then followed a statement of the relation of music to the new movement. "The music teaching of the future will be based on this truth, that if we would find the most profitable line for music in the schools we can do no better than to take as a guide the best that musical experience does for men and women in actual life: and that on the other hand, the results of schooling will have vital meaning in the ultimate lives of men and women just in proportion as the processes have vital meaning in the immediate lives of boys and girls."

"The best that music can do is to reach the heart, enrich emotional experience, and thus not only broaden the sympathies for social life, but also create a rarer atmosphere for the life of the spirit. This is true of school life no less than that later life for participation in whose duties and pleasures school aims to prepare."

The platform of Mr. Hayden's publication was:—

"First—An independent journal published in the interest of public school music. Its columns open for the full discussion of all phases of school-music, and methods of teaching the same."

"Second—To act as the organ of the Department of Music of the National Educational Association, and to assist in and record the work of the various committees of that body, and of the National Federation of School Music Teachers."

"Third—To secure a large staff of contributors among supervisors, superintendents and musicians and to present in each issue papers on various topics pertaining to school-music from their pens; also print a good portrait of the writer with each article contributed."

"Fourth—To arrange a series of biographical sketches of the supervisors of the country, beginning with the older ones, like Mason, Loomis, Holt, Blackman, Jepson, Stewart, and Hodgdon, following with the younger men in the profession, each article to be illustrated by portrait."

"Fifth—To print programs of graduating and other music performed in public by school choruses, and such personal items, changes of location of supervisors, etc., as might prove of interest to subscribers."

"Sixth—To print, several weeks before the date needed for use, new music suitable for the special occasions of Thanksgiving, Christmas, Washington's Birthday, Lincoln's Birthday, Memorial Day, Bird Day, Mother's Day and songs of the season."

"Seventh—To act as a medium of intercourse between the music supervisors of America and to assist in improving the condition of music in the public schools."

"In General—The journal would endeavor to be the friend of all publishing houses, but the servant of none, and of all supervisors, but the exponent of no clique."

To this platform Mr. Hayden consistently and successfully adhered.   He never omitted an issue of the magazine, nor did he ever show pettiness or partiality.   Particularly during its first fifteen years the magazine was an indispensable agent in unifying the school-music profession.   In a very real sense, every supervisor of music came to feel a personal relation to *School Music Monthly*.   Through its columns they became acquainted with each other's point of view, learned of significant happenings in all parts of the country, and were given full reports of important meetings and announcements of programs of meetings which were to take place.   For the first time it gave an opportunity to reach the attention of the entire school-music field for such leaders as Weaver, Howard, Jepson, Baldwin, Gowen, Rix, Giddings, Congdon, Frances E. Clark, Julia Ettie Crane, Helen Place, Tomlins, Fullerton, Dann, Miessner, Farnsworth, Earhart, McConathy and others who were making significant contributions to school-music methods.   In fact its pages contain the essential history of the profession since 1900, and through its historical articles much that went before.

In 1902 Mr. Hayden and Miss Place joined forces, and merged their separate magazines into one publication, *School Music Monthly*, with Helen Place as assistant editor.   With the January issue of 1908 the name was changed to *School Music* and never again changed.

The new attitude, which tended to make the subject matter of education the direct outcome of the child's interest as a member of society, came partly as a result of changing conditions in our national life, in the direction of complexity of human relationships. Our vast industrial expansion, increasing with each succeeding decade and enhanced by the Spanish-American War had brought about successive adaptions in economic and social living. Millions of families moved from rural communities to the cities. The multiplication of modern conveniencies not only affected the physical conditions of home life, but started the migratory movement of families into the modern apartment house. The education which the boy or girl formerly obtained from doing chores was no longer possible. The traditions of parental discipline tended to relax. Corporal punishment disappeared from the public school; and in its place was substituted a self-discipline motivated by the interest of the pupil in his school work. Hence the need of a new evaluation of subject matter in terms of this interest. Largely through the leadership of John Dewey the schools became less academic and more human.

A new conception of the meaning of community life in terms of social fellowship found expression in proposals to use the school house as a community center; and the idea of community singing, dormant since the old time singing-schools, was reborn. The new focus of attention upon the child also brought about the movement which has resulted in parent-teacher associations.

The last fifteen years of the nineteenth century saw the old book-subject curriculum, both elementary and secondary, begin to change in both subject matter and method. Drawing, clay modeling, color work, nature study, sewing, cooking and manual training made their way into the elementary schools and the sciences and the manual and home-arts into the high schools. The broadening conception of the function of the public school to provide training in vocational occupations resulted in the building of manual training high schools.

Meanwhile America had been growing up musically. Symphony orchestras steadily increased in number; the Boston Symphony, the Theodore Thomas Orchestra, the Pittsburgh, Cincinnati and Damrosch Orchestras and the concert band of Philip Sousa toured the country repeatedly, leaving behind them pulsating emotions and the stirring of musical ambitions. The Kneisel and other string quartets revealed the beauties of chamber music as the Listemann Quartet and the Mendelssohn Quintet Club had done before them. Concerts by world famous singers, violinists and pianists, including such artists as Melba, Kubelik and Paderewski reached every section of the country. Our American composers, Macdowell, Chadwick, Parker, Foote and others had gained recognition at home and abroad. The multiplication of conservatories and colleges of music made it unnecessary for the American student to go to Europe for foundational music study. Acquaintance with music was also immensely accelerated by the perfecting of the phonograph and the player-piano. These inventions brought the great music of the world within reach of every household, and the renditions of great artists became as familiar to the remote countryside as to the crowded concert halls of the cities.

No single musical influence was greater upon the whole country than that of Theodore Thomas, first in New York, later in Chicago, and from first to last making long tours with his orchestra. His programs, covering a period of forty years, and arranged to give the people not what they wanted but what they could understand, with standards gradually rising as his audiences grew in appreciation, show his method of making good music popular. His own philosophy of popular music is thus expressed by himself ;—"What is popular music?   The man who never enters a concert hall answers, 'It is music like *The Star Spangled Banner* or *Home Sweet Home*, or *Marching Through Georgia*, stirring, familiar strains such as we all know and love.'   A second man, who went to the old summer night concerts of by gone years will reply, 'It is music like the *Largo*, the *Spring Song*, *Traumerei*, tender flowers of melody which touch our hearts and which we know and love.'   Still a third, more advanced than the foregoing, will say, 'It is music like Beethoven's immortal *Fifth Symphony*, great thought expressed in simple, direct form, which appeals alike to heart and brain, and which we all know and love.'

"And thus, as a musician recently said in my hearing, 'you will always find that each person will describe as popular music that which is most familiar to him, and if all the symphonies were as familiar to the general public as the compositions just mentioned, they would at once be classed as popular music.' "[1]

The combination of influences which have been mentioned, educational, sociological and musical, pointed toward the twentieth century conception of the aim and purpose of music education, namely, appreciation.   The whole change in educational attitude and outlook came to be known as "The New Education," concerning which Edwin E. Slosson, in his book, *The American Spirit in Education*, writes as follows;—

"To a great extent the new education is new only in the sense that the school now teaches what once was learned outside its walls.   The twentieth century lad who learns at school to swim, to play ball, to build bird houses, to care for a vegetable garden, or to mend a broken lock, and girl who studies cooking, sewing, housework, first aid to the injured, and piano practice, may graduate no wiser than the children of a past generation who did all these things on the farm and went to school for a few weeks in winter to learn spelling and copper-plate penmanship. The new methods in education are largely based on principles that have been the commonplaces of educational theorists for generations."

The new emphasis upon song singing mentioned at the beginning of the chapter came as a reaction against over emphasis upon note reading to the comparatively neglect of the former. The assertion often made that if children are taught to read music, they will have in their possession a key to all its treasures is indisputable. And it is also true that the same attention to song singing on the expressive side, resulting in a large repertory of songs, if learned with the book in hand, will make readers of some of the children. But there is no evidence that our forefathers who introduced music into the public schools thought of either singing or sight reading as paramount one to the other; they were rather to re-enforce each other; both had an equal share in the larger conception of the musical development of the nation.

The new interest in chorus singing was largely set in motion by the work of William L. Tomlins with children. He was born in London, England, in 1844, studied as a choir boy with Macfarren and Silas, and

came to this country in 1870. After teaching in
New York he went to Chicago, and in 1873 became
director of the Apollo Club, which under his leadership grew into an eminent choral organization. His
remarkably effective interpretations of oratorios attracted wide attention to the guiding philosophy of
his choral methods, and led to his being asked to apply
these methods to children.

As early as 1883 he began training children's
choruses recruited from some of the poorer districts
of Chicago. The work soon grew to include large
training classes for teachers. National attention
was aroused to Mr. Tomlins' extraordinary effect
upon children at the time of the Columbian Exposition at Chicago in 1893. Concerts were given by a
chorus of 1500 children under his direction. The
spontaneity, sincerity and rare expressiveness of this
singing made a deep impression. The music itself
set a new standard in its expression of the feelings of
childhood, and, collected under the title *Columbian
Song Book* it made its way into many public schools.

In 1898, after a service of twenty-five years
Mr. Tomlins gave up his leadership of the Apollo
Club to devote his life to the music education of
children. From that time to the present he has
traveled extensively in this country and in England,
delivering his message from the lecture platform to
audiences of grade teachers, music supervisors and
school superintendents, and giving countless demon-

strations with classes of boys and girls. His influence upon school-music has been far reaching. To him, at least, more than to any other one person, the new emphasis upon spiritual values in music education was due.

The following is a summary of his philosophy in his own words;—"The trouble with our common school education is that it is concerned too exclusively with the things of knowledge, and that it leaves the deepest powers in the children undeveloped. This unused part is his spirit; the realm of Motive and Creative Life. The boy whose powers are merely physical is but a fraction of his true self. Add his mental powers and still you have only half your boy, for besides what he knows and does there is what he *is*. To fully fit your child for life, then, you must complete him; body, mind and spirit. Already his physical and lower-mind powers are active. Now awaken his intellectual and spiritual ones. Make him alive in his inner and innermost being, and soon he will pulse with the great world-life all about him, soon he will be filled with the joy of living, tireless in energy, just as when—a little fellow—he was in touch with his little play-world."

"In bringing this three-fold power of the child into harmonious expression you complete the circle of his individuality. Almost instantly there will come to him the awareness of this fuller life within and all around him. It is simply a question of completeness; of a complete bell which rings out its life, as against a cracked one which cannot and whose voice is but a dead chink."

"The effects of this transformation come quickly to view and are seen in self-reliance, initiative, purposefulness and many other things which make for character building.   In a word, the child's powers are approached from within as well as without, and thereby he is lifted so above and beyond his former powers as to be out of all comparison with them."

One of the first expositions of the principles underlying the song method was given in 1900 at the Charleston meeting of the music section of the N. E. A. by C. H. Congdon.   The following paragraphs are from his address ;—

"I desire to prove that in music, song is the basis of the child's study.   It first arouses his interest, and then fills his mind with musical forms and melodic concepts, which are the necessary foundation to his musical growth."

"Sight singing is largely an act of memory. The reader discovers through the notation, melodic progressions with which he is already familiar.   The notes suggest to the mind musical concepts already acquired through practice and experience.   These concepts must primarily be acquired by rote.   In order to fill the mind with melodic types of the most desirable quality, the learner must have a vital experience with the highest forms of melody.   After a rich song experience, the child should be brought to a closer observation of the constructive elements of the melody. This can be done by calling his attention to typical forms with which he has already had an unconscious experience, so far as the constructive elements are concerned. This unconscious song experience may be likened to his first experience with his mother tongue. A child learns to talk before he can begin to read. A great deal of the knowledge acquired by children through their perceptive faculties remains at first in the subconsciousness, and later on this knowledge becomes more definite and useful, but many of these subconscious impressions are the most firmly fixed in the memory. While practice in reading simple language prepares the child for the more difficult exercises, his first efforts in reading are based on the knowledge of language he has already acquired. This knowledge was acquired through vital experience, and in no other way. When a child is learning to talk his efforts are always preceded and inspired by thought which is born of the little experiences of his daily life. Whatever practice or drill he gets is always directly associated with this thought. The thought and the experience come first, and the practice afterward, and is based on the thought and experience. Now, every successful teacher knows that this principle is applied to teaching the child to read. The words and phrases requiring special drill are always selected from sentences presenting some thought in which the child is interested."

"So far as I am able to understand the new education, it means the renaissance of art, music and literature for the children. It calls for a better understanding of child nature, and of the things best suited to his proper development; it means freedom from dead processes, and the emancipation from cut and dried methods; it is the natural growth and unfolding of the child's faculties through wholesome effort stimulated by a vital interest in the things that interest him for good." . . . .

"It must be borne in mind that there are two kinds of drill necessary in teaching sight reading. The first I have already described; that is, the singling out of one or more of the constructive elements of a melody that is being studied, and re-iterating it for the purpose of fixing it in the mind. The second kind of drill is more general. It means the general practice of reading at sight. This kind of drill involves the use of simple, progressive melodies, and the important thing to be looked after is the use at all times of the very best that can be selected from musical literature."[1]

These were the underlying principles of the *Modern Music Series,* which was the joint production of Robert Foresman and Eleanor Smith, and published in 1898 by Scott, Foresman and Company.

[1]*School Music Monthly*—March, 1901.

In 1901 the publishing rights were acquired by Silver, Burdett and Company. The course of study for the new books was planned by Robert Foresman, and the governing psychology was his, but the general editorship of the series was the work of Eleanor Smith, who passed upon all the material, translated many of the most charming verses, and herself wrote many of the songs.

The *Modern Music Series* soon became extraordinarily popular, especially in the middle section of the country. Its psychology accorded well with that of the new education, and wherever this was in the ascendent the books made their way. It was the embodiment of the child-study movement in the field of music. The songs were buoyant, and appealed to the joyous spirit of childhood; many of them were little masterpieces of melody and style. As a compilation of song literature for children the series introduced a new era and set up a new standard. The pedagogy of the *Modern* books was frankly experimental and suggestive in its method rather than dogmatic. It left much to the judgment, the imagination and skill of the teacher. In its assertion that the song contains all the elements necessary for a reading technique, and that the songs must be of the highest quality, the *Modern Music Series* was a pioneer.

The new interest in song as a basis for music reading found further expression in the *Congdon*

Music Readers, edited and published by C. H. Congdon, the *Congdon Music Rolls,* by the same author, *The Song Series,* edited by Alys Bentley, of Washington, D. C., and the *Laurel Music Books,* edited by W. L. Tomlins.   Jessie Gaynor, Otto Miessner, Fannie Snow Knowlton and others enriched children's music literature with hundreds of songs which helped to satisfy the cravings of childhood for a genuine expression of its own rather than that of adult feeling.   Clarence C. Birchard published the *Laurel Books,* and added successively collections and separate songs which grew to be a veritable literature in itself, expressing the dominant feelings of childhood and youth.   This great outpouring of children's songs, in respect of their character and quality might appropriately be called the *Renaissance* of school music.

The period which this chapter covers extended from about 1895 to about 1910.   The child study movement which came to a head during this era and which brought about the "new education," effected an enlargement of the curriculum, bringing in additional studies in both the grades and high school. It also radically changed the spirit and method of teaching every subject.   In music this change of attitude produced the song method, which has gradually come to be accepted in some form by the generality of music supervisors.

During this entire period, however, many different theories were held as to how music should be taught. There were a small number who believed in the fixed DO method; many believed in the importance of teaching the details of notation even in the first and second grades; probably the majority adhered to teaching the key of C first, and following this by a succession of sharp and flat keys; nearly all believed that ear training should precede eye training, some, like Sterrie A. Weaver, separating tonal and rhythmic presentation before combining them, and some, like Philip C. Hayden, combining them from the beginning in one operation; finally there were the radicals who held that the rote song contained all the elements for teaching music. There certainly was a tendency to change keys oftener than formerly, and this helped to bring into general use the Congdon chromatic pitch pipe, which replaced the old C pipe with formulas for finding the various key tones.

There were also conflicting views regarding the aims of public school music teaching. One view was that teaching music reading was the sole concern of the music teacher, and that every thing else was secondary. The opposite was expressed by Samuel W. Cole at the Boston meeting of the N. E. A. in 1903, in the following summary;—

"The real purpose of teaching music in the public schools is not to make expert sight singers nor individual soloists. I speak from experience. I have done all these things and I can do them again; but I have learned that, if they become an end and not a means, they hinder rather than help, because they represent only the abilities of the few.   A much nobler, grander, more inspiring privilege is yours and mine; to get the great mass to singing and to make them love it."

It was part of the mission of the new education to blend these two view points, and to show that children could learn to read music without destroying a love for singing, and further that properly directed song singing would help rather than hinder music reading.

CHAPTER VII

THE TWENTIETH CENTURY

THE most striking characteristic of public school music as it has developed in the twentieth century is its many-sidedness. It is no longer exclusively vocal as in the past, although singing is still the fundamental musical activity. The aims of school-music teaching have shifted considerably from epoch to epoch, but always in the direction of values more and more clearly musical. In the introductory period the aim was to have every child learn to sing, and the values most thought of were those of recreation following mental fatigue from other studies. In the next generation the aim was to have every child learn to read music because this power is the key to an understanding of its treasures, a value which was concerned mainly with the child's future. The child-study movement was largely responsible for making clear the present aim of school-music, which is that every child shall appreciate and take pleasure in music, not in a vague and indefinite future, but here and now.

Doubtless from the beginning this latter aim had

some significance in music teaching, but not until one generation had proved that all children could learn to sing and another that all could learn to read music did it become clear that both of these desirable abilities were but means or accompaniments of the real aim—a joy in music as music—for which there seems no more fitting term than the general word appreciation, or, as concretely stated in the *Fourth Year Book* of the Department of Superintendence, "The specific or musical aim is to develop appreciation of the beauty that is in music."   Thus we see that today the music educator is building his teaching procedure upon purely musical foundations, upon that quality of music, namely, beauty of tone, which it shares with no other subject.

The new point of view was a concomitant of the emphasis upon singing which came at the turn of the century.   It was confirmed and strengthened continually by the results of child study upon educational theory and practice.   That knowledge comes not by being poured in but by doing desirable things which are motivated by the child's intrinsic interest was a discovery as momentous to school-music as to education in general.   It is our best guide to an understanding of the schools of today and particularly of music teaching.   It helps to account for an ever increasing emphasis upon democracy in education and for an enriched and changing curriculum, and in the case of music, for the addition one after

another of new activities and interests.   In studying
the progress of school-music during the last quarter-
century it has seemed wise to consider separately the
most important phases of its development.

High School Music

The development of music in the high school as
a serious study has taken place almost wholly within
the present century, and mostly within the last fifteen
years.   But the foundations for this development
were laid in the last decades of the nineteenth century,
at which time the results of sight reading in the
grades began to show in the ability of high schools
to produce standard choral works.

Some early performances of oratorios were mentioned in a former chapter.   To these may be added
two renditions of *The Creation*, both given in the
year 1903, one at Somerville, Massachusetts, under
the leadership of S. Henry Hadley, and the other at
Northampton, Massachusetts, under the direction of
Ralph L. Baldwin.   Early in the century also a large
number of high schools were preparing and performing such works as Cowen's *Rose Maiden*, Gaul's *Holy
City* and *Ruth*, Anderton's *Wreck of the Hesperus*,
and Lahee's *The Building of the Ship*.   These choral
accomplishments were not limited to any one section
of the country.   They were widely scattered, and in
some cases the high school chorus were reinforced
by adult voices.   These choral performances were

regarded as the crowning fulfillment of the work in the grades. No one then dreamed of the way in which instrumental study was soon to enlarge the scope of school-music.

The results of instrumental study under private teachers began, however, before 1900 to take other forms than solo playing, and we find groups of young instrumentalists here and there forming orchestras, like that in the high school of Aurora, Illinois, organized in 1878 by B. W. Merrill, then a student in the school.

In his grammar school days the writer was a member of a boys' orchestra of ten players, which played at the graduation in 1883. They also played at a concert in which all the schools took part. This group was a social organization which practiced evenings at the homes of the members, and without a director. Such groups as those mentioned were probably formed in a similar manner in other communities at about the same time.

Toward the close of the century orchestras began to be organized upon a more permanent basis, such as those formed in 1896 at Wichita, Kansas, by Jessie Clark, in 1898 at Richmond, Indiana, by Will Earhart, and the same year at the Manual Training High School of Indianapolis by Charles E. Emmerich, principal of the school. Grammar school orchestras were started in 1896 by Charles B. Jennings at New London, Connecticut, and in 1899 by W. D. Monnier at Hartford, Connecticut.

Closely coincident in time with the beginnings of orchestras were those of music appreciation as a definite type of study.   Near the turn of the century Frances E. Clark organized music history courses for the high school at Ottumwa, Iowa, Peter Dykema introduced the pupils of the Fletcher School in Indianapolis to a study of the operas of Richard Wagner, Will Earhart started critical study courses at Richmond, Indiana, and Mary Regal her appreciation courses in the high schools of Springfield, Massachusetts.   In 1899, Frederick E. Chapman added harmony, counterpoint and melody writing to the music curriculum of the high school of Cambridge, Massachusetts.

The early stages of secondary school-music development were complicated with the question of crediting the work, especially of applied music. The long hallowed tradition that music is an accomplishment rather than a serious study made the principals of high schools cautious in dealing with the question at a time when the disciplinary value of the old curriculum was still the deciding factor in estimating credit values.   During this period applied music was on trial, so to speak, and had to prove its worth.

These pioneer efforts to enlarge the field of music study pushed into the foreground the whole question

of the secondary school-music curriculum, and led to
a conference in Boston, in 1902, called by the New
England Education League.   A committee was appointed to draw up a major music course for high
schools, with Hamilton C. Macdougall, of Wellesley
College as chairman.   An elective course in music was
formulated providing for "four hours of music each
week of the four high school years, a total (counting
thirty-six weeks to the year) of 576 hours.   Piano,
voice, organ, or instrument of the symphony orchestra to be credited as laboratory work.   The
customary period of choral work added to the above
make five periods per week, with ensemble as an
alternative in the fourth year."[1]

The course was comprehensive and was planned
tc be taught by well qualified teachers to serious
minded students.   In addition to the courses in applied music it provided for elementary and advanced
harmony, counterpoint and form, and musical bio-
graphy and history.   The courses were so arranged
that the first two years could constitute an elementary
course, and under certain conditions the entire program could be completed in three years.   This was
the first constructive attempt to organize high school
music as a major study and on a regular credit basis.
It received the endorsement of the Music Teachers
National Association and the Music Section of the
N. E. A. in 1904.

[1]*N. E. A. Proceedings*—Music Section—1904.

The provisions in this report, however, for instruction in piano and orchestra instruments were impossible of attainment at this early period; but it led to an agitation of the question of crediting such work pursued under private teachers, and in 1906 a committee from The New England Education League under the chairmanship of Leo R. Lewis formulated a plan for crediting such music study. This in effect was an amendment of the music course planned by the Macdougall committee, and without which the courses in applied music would have been largely a dead letter. It provided for an introductory examination in sight reading and ear training before enrolling in the course, and for collateral work in theory, as well as monthly reports of the work of the pupil and for semester and yearly examinations. Two credit points were allowed for one recitation per week coupled with one hour's daily preparation (the latter making five hours per week considered as laboratory work).

Closely related with these questions was that of granting college entrance credits for music pursued in secondary schools, and through the efforts of The New England Education League the College Entrance Examination Board for New England and the Middle States voted in 1906 to add music to the list of subjects for entrance examinations.

The first school system to adopt the high school music course in complete detail, together with its outside credit provisions was that of Chelsea, Massachusetts, in 1906, under the direction of Osbourne McConathy.   The Chelsea plan attracted wide attention on account of its comprehensiveness and particularly on account of its outside credit features, which made instrumental work possible as a regular study.

Perhaps no one thing has done more to bring together music supervisors and private teachers than their common interest over the latter question.   It was argued that, granting the educational value of such study, and considering the fact that the parent is willing to tax himself to pay for instruction which the school is not equipped to furnish, full academic credit should be given for the work under the same restrictions as to quality and standards as prevail in the school.   It was shown that musically talented high school students who were studying piano or violin were frequently compelled to choose between leaving school and continuing their music, or remaining in school and dropping music.   The combination of from one to four hours of practice added to three or four hours of study of other subjects made a prohibitively heavy load.   The principle involved was clearly stated in the government bulletin, No. 40, prepared by Will Earhart and Osbourne McConathy, and entitled *Music in Secondary Schools*, as follows;—"We regard as untenable the assumption, expressed or implied, that any individual would be uneducated if he pursued three or four regular studies per year and added music to these, but would be educated if he pursued four or five studies each year and dropped music. We believe that this untenable assumption is due not to any active consideration of the question as to the place of music in an educational plan, but rather to a passive acceptance of traditional academic standards that are now outgrown and should be abandoned."

During the decade following its first adoption in Chelsea the principle of outside credits was put into operation in many cities. The problem of checking up on the work of the pupil, however, and of handling monthly reports, of providing for semi-annual examinations and other details of administration, have had enough deterrant effect to keep the plan from universal adoption, especially in small communities. Nevertheless, the merits of the idea are so clear, and its justice to the private pupil's interest so undeniable, that several states, including New York, Pennsylvania and Indiana have given the plan authoritative sanction, with regulatory restrictions for the maintenance of standards. The latest pronouncement on the subject was formulated in Bulletin *No. 2*, prepared by the National Research Council of Music Education of the Music Supervisors National Conference, and adopted by that body in 1922 for standard use.

Though the first attempts to enrich the secondary school-music curriculum were scattering, they did not long remain isolated.   They were soon followed by others, especially in the cities where the elective system was most advanced, so that by 1910 the frame work of the present secondary school program, including chorus, orchestra, harmony and appreciation became plainly visible over the country at large, the most striking feature of this advance being the rapid spread of instrumental work.

In the last fifteen years has occurred a forward movement in school-music entirely without precedent. The list of musical studies and activities in the curriculum of a high school of the first rank reads very much like that of a high-grade conservatory of music. In the vocal field there are mixed chorus, boys' and girls' glee-clubs and classes in vocal technique; the instrumental field includes first and second orchestras and bands and classes for instruction in all instruments, including the piano; in theory there are classes in harmony, counterpoint and composition, and the list includes also music-appreciation and history, with a strong swing toward making appreciation compulsory for all students.   The choruses practice and perform in public the standard oratorios, the glee clubs sing part songs, cantatas and light operas, and the orchestras play the symphonies of Haydn, Mozart and Beethoven and many of the best overtures and

suites, both classic and modern. The bands are of
symphonic fulness in instrumentation and perform
the standard selections of band literature. The ensembles include also string quartets and other cham-
ber-music groups.

This combined achievement, though bewildering
from the rapidity with which it has taken place, is not
difficult to account for. It is due on the one hand
to the intense enthusiasm of adolescence for playing
instruments and participating with others in musical
performance, and on the other to the practical application of the principle that every child is entitled
to the kind of music education which accords with his
talents and inclinations as a part of his public school
course, and above all to the increasing encouragement
and support of boards of education, school administrators and the community at large. Another contributing cause of great importance is the change
from the former eight years of elementary and four
years of high school with little or no co-ordination,
to the six year elementary, three year junior and
three year senior high school with a high degree of
co-ordination. This reorganization has helped to
keep many children in school who under former conditions would have dropped out at the end of the
eighth grade, and together with the compulsory age
limit has caused a quadrupling of high school attendance within the last two decades.

Music in the Elementary Grades

The principal development in methods of teaching in the last quarter-century has been in the direction of simplification of procedure. The song method, which was received with caution at first, has been generally accepted in principle, and today it forms the basis of most of the teaching of music reading. Much of the time formerly spent in drilling on the scale and various details of notation now goes into more music reading, on the principle of learning to do by doing. Difficulties of tone and rhythm which once were anticipated by preliminary drill are now dealt with as they occur in the song context, and with the smallest possible interruption to the rhythmic flow of the music.

The enrichment of the music curriculum beyond the former solitary singing activity has not been confined to the secondary school. A somewhat similar broadening of the field of music study has taken place in the elementary grades since the second decade of the century. Then began the spread of music appreciation in the form of listening lessons in all the lower schools, and in the primary grades much use of song games and folk dances. The violin class movement began in the intermediate grades and prepared the way for grammar school orchestras which now are a regular part of the curriculum of a majority of elementary schools. Very recently toy rhythmic orchestras have come into considerable vogue in the primary grades, and their development is in the direction of their extension upward, gradually making use of violins and other instruments, thus preparing the children for regular participation in orchestra work.   Within the last decade the music memory contest has come into wide use, with a vitalizing effect upon music study and helping to motivate the study of music appreciation.

The song material for the elementary grades has been enriched by the publication of many courses of music readers.   The *Modern Music Series*, by Eleanor Smith was published in 1898.   Following this in chronological order came—

1903-1906   *The New Educational Music Course,* by James McLaughlin, George A. Veazie and W. W. Gilchrist, published by Ginn and Company.

1908   *The Eleanor Smith Music Series,* by Eleanor Smith, published by The American Book Company.

1912   *The Lyric Music Series,* by Arthur Edward Johnstone, Harvey Worthington Loomis and William A. White, published by Scott, Foresman and Company.

1915   *The Hollis Dann Music Course,* by Hollis Dann, published by The American Book Company.

1915   *The Progressive Music Series,* by Horatio W. Parker, Osbourne McConathy, W. Otto Miessner and Edward B. Birge, published by Silver, Burdett and Company.

1920   *The Universal Music Series,* by Walter
            Damrosch, Karl W. Gehrkens and George
            Gartlan, published by Hinds, Hayden and
            Eldridge.

1923   *The Music Education Series,* by Thaddeus P.
            Giddings, Will Earhart, Ralph L. Baldwin and
            Elbridge W. Newton, published by Ginn and
            Company.

1923   *The Foresman Books of Songs,* by Robert
            Foresman, published by The American Book
            Company.

1925   *A One Book Course in Elementary Music,* by
            Charles A. Fullerton, published by Fullerton
            and Gray.

1927   *The Music Hour Series,* by Osbourne
            McConathy, W. Otto Miessner, Edward B.
            Birge and Mabel E. Bray, published by
            Silver, Burdett and Company.

THE INSTRUMENTAL DEVELOPMENT

The belated entrance of instrumental music into
the curriculum of the public schools was due to a
variety of causes. One of the most fundamental of
these was the continuance throughout much of the
nineteenth century of the early prejudice against
secular as opposed to sacred music, a prejudice
carried over from the previous century. During the
seventeenth century instrumental music was non-
existent in the colonies. In the eighteenth century
pipe organs began to appear in the churches, and
instrumental music began to have a place as a social

diversion, but its serious cultivation was generally regarded as frivolous if not wicked. This general attitude cast its shadow over three quarters of the nineteenth century, as shown in the conservative feeling that instrumental study was no part of the serious business of living. Piano playing did not share in this prejudice, this being generally regarded as a fitting accomplishment, especially for young women.

But whether the feeling regarding instruments was one of suspicion or indifference, it was due to lack of opportunity to hear master works played with authority and distinction. It was not until the middle of the century, when all sections of the country heard Ole Bull, Remenyi, Camilla Urso and The Germania Orchestra, that the American people awoke to a realization of what they had been missing. Between that time and the present all of our remarkable orchestral development has taken place, with the balance moving strongly at present toward a preponderance of instrumental over vocal ensembles.

There were other incidental causes which delayed the beginnings of public school instrumental work. One of these was doubtless the fact that most of the music supervisors were not instrumentalists, but singers, with the singer's point of view. Another reason was the attitude of school principals and superintendents. There had been no precedent for instrumental work in the schools either of this country or even of Europe.   Chamber music was widely cultivated in the family circles of Germany, and every town had its orchestra, but school-music in this and the other European countries was confined to singing and the study of the rudiments.   The introduction of vocal music into our public schools was largely influenced by the singing in the schools of Europe. Not so with instrumental music; its entrance into the schools was due to conditions inherent in the growth of democracy in education, which developed an elective system giving the pupil a free choice of a wide range of studies.

The apparently spontaneous impulse in various communities, especially in the Middle West to organize orchestras in the high schools began about the year 1900.   These early organizations were all extraneous activities, with no settled place in the school program, and were forced to hold their rehearsals after school hours.   Their membership was made up of pupils of private teachers.   Instrumentation at best was limited to that of the ordinary theatre orchestra, namely, first and second violins, an occasional bass and cello, cornets, trombones, clarinets, flutes, drums and piano.   There were always plenty of violins and cornets, and it was not usually difficult to secure an occasional clarinet and trombone or flute, but basses and cellos were scarce, and there were no violas, French horns, oboes, bassoons or kettle drums.

With such varying equipment orchestras of
twenty or more players began to be fairly numerous
early in the century. The purpose of the supervisors
who organized these first orchestras did not include
teaching instrumental technique, nor even less of
starting an orchestra of beginners. They chose boys
and girls who already possessed creditable playing
ability, and welded them into as perfect an ensemble
as the varying capacities of the players permitted.
The result was a magnified nine-piece orchestra in
variety of instruments, playing a repertory of
marches, waltzes, operatic arrangements and standard overtures. Programs chosen from such material
were given at school assemblies, commencement exercises and at public concerts of the music department.
These opportunities for public performance afforded
an additional stimulus for the youthful players to
practice diligently at rehearsals, besides giving the
people a new idea of school-music possibilities. The
home public quickly gave unqualified approval to
their school orchestra and were glad to have their
children enrolled therein; while the larger public of
the county and state teachers' associations, for whose
program they were frequently asked to furnish the
music, afforded an effective means of advertising to
the school world the practical value of the new
activity. The desire of many superintendents and
school principals was thus aroused to introduce orchestras into their own schools. By the end of the

first decade the movement had spread to many cities and towns of the Middle West. Orchestral organization became early very active also in California, notably in Los Angeles, and the movement began at the same time to make headway in the Atlantic states.

The status of the high school orchestra was not at first that of an accredited subject. The attitude of the principals was cordial to it as an extra-curricula activity, and they valued the added prestige the orchestras gave their schools, but they did not see in them enough educational value to justify putting them on an accredited basis. It was at least a decade and a half before they won a place in the curriculum with rehearsals taking place during school hours and with credit given for the work. By that time, indeed, the orchestra contagion had spread far and wide, and had gained general acceptance as something desirable and worth while. In fact from the inception of the instrumental movement in the schools there has been no retrogression or curtailment in its activities, but on the contrary a constant and rapid growth.

In an article written for *School Music* in 1905, Will Earhart, then supervisor of music at Richmond, Indiana, gives a faithful picture of the high school orchestra at that period. Mr. Earhart was one of the first to expand the high school music curriculum beyond merely vocal activities, by adding harmony, appreciation and orchestra. He had also the unique experience of developing the orchestra at Richmond

between the years 1898 and 1912 from a small group
of a dozen players to an organization with full symphonic equipment. The following quotation is from
the article referred to;—

"This organization (the orchestra) meets after
school hours—from four to five-thirty or six—once a
week, with extra rehearsals during or after school
hours when they are needed. Half a credit a semester
is given and pupils are admitted who can show sufficient ability. Occasionally pupils are permitted to
rehearse before their ability is adequate to playing
in public performance, but these do not receive credits
until regularly admitted. The board of education
provides the music, and this has entailed no increase
in expense, as formerly it cost the board a large sum
each year for orchestras for the two annual commencements, while now only one or two professionals,
who are brought in to fill gaps in our instrumentation,
need to be hired. Besides the commencements the
orchestra plays regularly for chapel exercises every
Monday morning, accompanying also, at this time,
the hymns sung by the school, provides music for the
annual junior and senior publics, making the expense
to members of these classes materially less, and plays
for the County Teachers' association, which meets
twice a year. Occasionally, also, it furnishes music
for lectures and other entertainments given before
the city corps of teachers or for the benefit of the
schools. No music work done has met with more

approbation from citizens, school officials and students than this of the orchestra. A strict standard is maintained as regards the quality of the music chosen and the individual and ensemble playing of the members, and the results have been very gratifying. The only discouraging feature is the constant changing of personnel and instrumentation brought about by members graduating from or quitting the school, but this is partially offset by the fact that the interest and appreciation of these members is usually so great as to lead them to come back and play with us, if they remain in town, at least whenever most needed, and often regularly, for a year or two after they have left the school. Last spring, for instance, we lost our one clarinet and our cello player, but these have both been with us, in the way described, during all of this year. With them our present instrumentation is four first violins, four seconds, cello, bass, three flutes, clarinet, drums and piano. The violin is my instrument, so I lead with that. Three flutes are, of course, not needed, but these players are exceptionally capable, and so the difficulty of keeping them in tune is not so great as might be imagined. The noticeable lack of brass instruments has persisted now for over a year, and is much regretted. Cornet and trombone have to be hired for all exceptional occasions on account of it, and it seriously hampers us in selecting music and in rehearsing. Before quitting this topic I should say that we could often have a larger instrumentation if we would make sacrifices in the quality of the music chosen or in the standard of performance, but I am not willing to do either of these things. Rather it is better to play good music and play it well with a thinner instrumentation. A greater difficulty is to find good music in which these instruments that we lack are not indispensable, but indefatigable searching will bring this. Once found, the absence of inefficient players is fully realized to be a blessing. Such numbers as Gounod's *Faust, Ballet Music (2d Suite)*, Cherubini's *Lodioska* overture, Carl Bohm's *Birthday Festival Music*, and Bellini's *Norma* overture—numbers that are among the best in our repertoire—demand, for musicianly performance, a clean technic and musical sense—and they should not be cast aside for cheaper pieces played with a larger instrumentation."[1]

It was undoubtedly fortunate for the future of the movement that the first orchestras could show immediate results in a commendable quality of performance. This fact enabled them to gain a favorable hearing. As early as 1905, however, forward looking supervisors were experimenting with the problem of adding basses, violas, horns, oboes, bassoons and kettle drums to their instrumentation. They accepted the fact that on account of the rarity of these instruments and their non solo qualities the parents were not willing to buy them, though they were ready to buy violins or cornets.   They therefore had recourse to the expedient of buying them for the school from the proceeds of concerts, or inducing the school authorities to allow an appropriation for them. In some cases they secured a donation from the local chamber of commerce for the purpose.   With instruments thus secured ambitious orchestras soon began to take on something like symphonic proportions. Basses and cellos were added, then violas, horns, and finally oboes, bassoons and tympani.

The question of how these instruments were to be taught was always acute, and an interesting story, borrowed from the experience of many supervisors might be written of the varying ways of accomplishing it.   Violinists were induced to take up the bass viol, cello, or viola, cornet players changed over to the French horn, and clarinet players to oboe and bassoon.   Wonders were done with instruction books coupled with adolescent enthusiasm.   Sometimes, to be sure, the pupils would receive instruction from resident private teachers.   The occasional visit of a symphony orchestra would be taken advantage of for a lesson from the artist oboist or bassoonist. Above all, and a fact of capital importance, the pupils passed on to each other in their own effective way what they learned.   In fact, no means were neglected for helping individual players acquire enough technique to take their place in the orchestra ensemble. At the time when the project method was beginning to be talked about, the high school orchestra, with its many absorbing problems for both teacher and student, presented a good practical illustration.

How widespread before the World War were the successful attempts to enlarge the instrumentation of the orchestra is a matter of conjecture.   The achievements thus far described are of a pioneer character. To create orchestras where none had existed before required enterprise and initiative, and doubly so to add the use of unfamiliar and unusual instruments. Among others of the pre-war period who worked at the problem and who did much to stimulate the forward movement, besides Will Earhart were Osbourne McConathy at Chelsea, Massachusetts, Hamlin E. Cogswell at Edinburg, Pennsylvania, James D. Price at Hartford, Connecticut, Anton H. Embs at New Albany, Indiana, Ralph Sloane at Sullivan, Indiana, and Glenn H. Woods, who began his work at Oakland, California shortly before the War.

From these foundational beginnings, there followed for instrumental music three lines of development, all having their inception at about the same time, namely, grade school orchestras, grade and high school bands, and instrumental class instruction. Though to some extent independent movements, they all grew out of the previous orchestra movement, or were developed as the solution of some phases of its problems.

It was apparent, for example, that a way must

be found to secure a more permanent personnel in the orchestra. With several players leaving school every year, especially from the wind instrument sections, anything approaching a permanent playing group became impossible. The solution was the grade school orchestra. The most resourceful leaders not only organized such orchestras, but began to purchase duplicate sets of instruments for the high and grade schools. Thus was started a plan of co-ordinated effort which made possible a continuous orchestral experience of six years or more, instead of the average two or three previously possible.

But though often organized to serve as feeders for the high school orchestra, they soon developed an independent activity on their own account, and began to multiply rapidly. Los Angeles reported thirty grade school orchestras in 1909, in 1915 there were forty in Kansas City, and the same year Oakland, California had twenty-nine, and an equal number of grade school bands.

Another result of the growing interest in instrumental playing was the school band movement, which began to attract attention from about 1910. Though often closely associated with the orchestra, either as an adjunct and source of supply for wind instruments, and though the same boys frequently played in both organizations, this activity more often started independently of the orchestra, the prevailing motive in many cases being to capitalize the irresistible appeal which bands, especially in uniform, make to the adolescent boy, and thus turn it into educational channels. The town band on parade or giving concerts in the public square was a familiar and joyous experience, and when the schools offered the boys a chance to form a band of their own they were more than ready. The fact also that there were more boys who played band instruments than the orchestras could absorb helped to facilitate band organization.

Unlike the orchestra, which began by selecting players of experience, the band had largely to develop playing ability from the ground up. W. Otto Miessner, while supervisor of music at Connersville, Indiana, organized such a band, teaching all the instruments himself. In *School Music* of March, 1909, he describes this experience. "One day we told the boys that we, with their co-operation, would organize a brass band—at first they were incredulous, then grew interested. It was explained to them that the better a boy's attitude toward the regular music work, the better his chances for acceptance into the band membership. Of course, not all of the boys were ambitious, but some of the 'gang leaders' were, and their change of attitude soon brought about a wholesome change for the better in the other boys. I arranged for fifteen-minute lesson periods with the boys whose parents had consented to buy instruments. These lessons I gave during the noon intermission and after school hours, and within two months I had twelve boys, which number was soon increased to eighteen, all of whom I taught individually and ensemble in this manner. The boys practiced and attended rehearsals faithfully, lured on by the goal set before them, which was a public concert and uniforms with caps of the high school colors. This year (1909) the number has been increased to thirty-two pieces with instruments worth in the aggregate over twelve hundred dollars."

"Our instrumentation is as follows; two piccolos, four clarinets, two saxophones, four solo cornets, two second cornets, two third cornets, four altos, four slide trombones, two baritones, two tubas and four drums. This array of instruments is enough to fill the uninitiated supervisor with alarm and apprehension, but it is really very simple when one learns that these can be reduced to about three classes, the mechanical manipulation of which is the same. A number of these boys come from the various grade buildings, in order to stimulate an interest in the grades, so that we now have a waiting list of twenty boys or more who have bought instruments and are learning to play, later on to take the places of the members who graduate or leave school. The age of the present members ranges from eleven to seventeen years."

The above typically illustrates the stores of courage, enthusiasm, tact, physical endurance and resourcefulness which were drawn upon to lay foundations in new and untried fields. Our supervisors could not wait for the miracle to happen of orchestras and bands springing up of their own accord. They had to perform this miracle themselves or not at all.

J. M. Thompson, the veteran music supervisor at Joliet, Illinois, describes in *School Music* of March, 1915, the beginning of band work in that city, and illustrating a somewhat later phase of the movement.

"In September of 1913 I went before the Board of Education, not asking for pianos or victors, but for a set of high grade band instruments. Four cornets, four clarinets, three slide trombones, three altos, two baritones, two E-flat tubas and two drums. I sent word to ten of our eight-room buildings for the sixth grade teacher to send me two boys of her class that stood the highest in average of all subjects and at the same time a good singer."

"An interesting group of sixth grade boys of English, Irish, Scotch, Italian, German, Swedish, Hungarian, Hebrew and Norwegian parentage. Not one had ever blown a toot. I told them I would see their parents about them joining a new school band. I placed each boy's name on a list and afterwards listed each boy to a horn according to my best judgment. I secured the help of a good trombone player to take the trombone boys, a good clarinet player for the clarinet boys and a general band master to help me with the rest of the three-valve horns."

"On the fifth day of October, 1913, the instruments arrived and the boys were sent for at 4 p.m.; they were seated in a circle and as each boy's name was called he came forward and accepted the horn I had assigned.   I told each boy to love his instrument for we could not have a band if everybody wanted the same kind of horn.   The trombone boys were sent to a room with their teacher.   The clarinets with theirs and the band master and I with the other fifteen.   They were shown at once how to blow and how to breathe.   The second week all played the scale from their little book.   I met them once a week alone as soon as they played in unison and my good helpers met them in groups once a week also.   The fifth week we played a little march.   And the eighth week a march, a waltz and America."

"Other boys joined (parents applied for admission for their boys) by purchasing their own instruments, and the number kept constantly increasing and at the end of our first year we had fifty-five members."

"Our uniforms consist of white duck military coats and white duck caps with blue bands lettered in gold.   We march through the business part of the city every Thursday at four o'clock escorted by two police officers.   We play for all community singing at the parks and schools and the municipal Christmas Tree."

"Our Township High School has always had a

very efficient orchestra and since our public school band has started, the high school has developed a remarkably good military band; and each year as we graduate the boys from the eighth grade we have qualified sixth grade boys ready to take the place of those who pass on and thereby make the band perpetual."

The fifteen years in which instrumental music was becoming established in the schools put to the test the ability of the American public school system to adjust itself to widening educational aims, purposes and ideals. During this interval the junior high school came into being, and the National Committee on the Reorganization of Secondary Education formulated a philosophy of adolescent educational development in harmony with the spirit of the period. It was an era of readjustment. School authorities found difficulty, not in sympathizing with and welcoming the participation of pupils in instrumental activities, but in accepting the material consequences involved, such as the purchase of instruments, supplying rooms for practice, employing additional teachers, and arranging their place in the curriculum. The constantly mounting proofs of its effectiveness as an educational subject and its almost literal invasion of the school room combined at last to bring about a general acceptance of instrumental instruction as a legitimate school activity and provision for its adequate development.

One of the logical consequences of the taking over by the schools of the development of orchestras and bands was the purchase of instruments as laboratory equipment, thus making the same provision in principle for music as for the departments of chemistry, physical science, home economics and shop work. An early and striking instance of such provision was that of Oakland, California, which in 1913 purchased instruments to the value of $10,000 and organized an instrumental teaching staff under the direction of Glenn Woods to give class instruction and develop a band and orchestra ensemble in every school. Closely following Oakland came Grand Rapids, Pittsburgh, Cleveland, Detroit and several other large cities with similar provisions. Then in 1918, George Eastman donated $15,000 worth of band and orchestra instruments to the City of Rochester, and thus made possible the extraordinary instrumental development of that city.

At the beginning and for several years the work of forming and conducting orchestras was done by the music supervisors themselves or, in the large cities, by the high school music teacher. There were then no school instrumental teachers or supervisors. But with the rapid spread of the movement and the growing realization that the future held unexpected possibilities in completeness of instrumentation and technical skill in performance came the conviction that special teachers were needed in instrumental technique and that the lessons must be given in the schools or at least under school authority. A beginning was usually made by part-time teaching, paving the way gradually for the full-time instrumental teacher and supervisor.

Meanwhile the development of the movement received an impetus from a somewhat similar situation which had arisen in the schools of England. Early in the twentieth century in the town of Maidstone the curate of the Parish Church started violin classes with the object of developing a love for orchestral playing among the pupils. The work was successful and soon spread to other districts and rapidly assumed large proportions. The attention of our supervisors was directed to this movement by Charles Farnsworth, who visited the schools of England in 1908, and wrote as follows regarding it;—"I heard a concert given by the school orchestras in and about London in Alexandra Palace, where fourteen hundred and fifty youthful instrumentalists took part. It is astonishing to see what can be done under these conditions. The idea of teaching the violin in classes strikes one at first as almost impossible, but here is a movement where just this thing is done, not in school time, but outside, yet under the direction of the school authorities. For instance, if a principal wishes to organize a school orchestra, he needs only to write to Murdock and Company, dealers in musical instruments, and they will supply him with circulars to distribute among the parents and will help him in organizing his classes. They will also supply the instruments and music, and even a teacher, if desired. The Murdock Company has probably sold nearly a half-million violins as the result of this movement in England, Scotland and Wales. At the same time they have stimulated musical endeavor in thousands of homes. . . . . Three half hours taken out of the noon recess is a common time for practice. As the same books and charts are used in all the orchestral classes, the child moving from one district to another loses nothing. In from six to eight months a beginner is able to play the accompaniments in the school music, and in the second year exhibit work may commence. It is estimated that in London alone there are over three hundred of these violin classes, with an average membership of twenty-five and that there is scarcely a town throughout England where there are not one or more classes."

In 1910 Albert G. Mitchell, then one of the music supervisors of the Boston schools, was given a year's leave of absence to study the violin class instruction in England. The result of this visit was the introduction of this work in the Boston schools, and the creation of the *Mitchell Class Method*, published by The Oliver Ditson Company, concerning which matters Dr. Mitchell writes as follows;—
"Upon my return home, in 1911, filled with enthusiasm and with a determination to do what I could

to keep pace with the activities in Europe, I received permission from the Boston School Board to organize violin classes upon my own responsibility and in my own time. They were held after school hours from four to five o'clock. No fees were asked. Five classes were formed, each having from sixteen to twenty pupils. The text books came from England. The children brought their own violins. Some had no bridges, many had no strings, and the bows in too many cases were of the shape familiar to Robin Hood. At the end of the school year a demonstration was given from which I learned many things. After the second year the director of music procured permission for me to leave my High School work, and to devote all my time to instrumental instruction."

"Classes were formed in many districts and were given a standing by being recognized as part of the regular school work. I gave a lesson once a week in all classes, and grade teachers were trained and paid to act as my assistants and to give a weekly review of my work. No expense was incurred by the pupils beyond providing their own violins. The books as authorized text-books were furnished by the city. A weekly practice card which had to be signed by the parent showed me whether the pupils had practiced half an hour each day at home."

"Very soon unexpected difficulties were encountered. The imported text-books, for example, failed to satisfy the desire for a sound pedagogical basis of teaching. The early training in normal school and university was ever recurring to me. It appeared imperatively necessary to devise a better text-book, so, with this in view, I spent much time and several quires of music paper in writing new exercises and pieces and trying them out in the class room to note the children's reaction. Thus, I wrote a *Class Method for the Violin*."

So began violin class-work in this country. The classes in Boston became widely known and were visited by many interested teachers from other places. Dr. Mitchell experimented with and adopted various mechanical aids to help to overcome some of the difficulties inherent to class instruction, such as non-slip pegs, metal first strings, paper finger-board charts and chin and shoulder rests. During the next decade the movement spread to all sections of the country, and class methods were applied not only to violin but to all band and orchestra instruments. Various ways of starting classes were resorted to, according to local conditions. Some supervisors made arrangements with private teachers of violin to take classes after school hours, the children paying a small fee per lesson. Others were able to secure an appropriation for instrumental teachers on a part-time basis. Still others, especially in the large cities, were fortunate in being able to add full-time instruction.

With the spread of class instruction instrumental work entered upon its second stage of development; and instead of aiming at producing individual players, the emphasis has been upon the ensemble idea—drilling the class as an orchestral section, strings, woodwind or brass—and combining them to form orchestras and bands.   The extraordinary success with which orchestras have been formed from instrumental classes is one of the unique features of the movement, which is nothing if not practical. Out of it has come a new technique of teaching, requiring on the part of the teacher the ability to give instruction in all instruments section-wise, together with a high degree of executive skill.   The large numbers of instrumental teachers who have thus entered the field of school-music have added strength and balance to the profession.

An important factor in holding the instrumental movement to a high standard of achievement has been the work of the instrumental committee of the Music Supervisors National Conference, consisting of Jay W. Fay, chairman, Victor L. F. Rebmann, B. F. Stuber, Russell V. Morgan, and Eugene Hahnel. This committee served from 1922 to 1925, when another committee was appointed consisting of Jay W. Fay, J. E. Maddy, Russell V. Morgan, Raymond N. Carr, Victor L. F. Rebmann and C. M. Tremaine. The following report of the committee, given in 1926, is instructive:—

"The Standing Committee on instrumental

affairs was appointed for two years at the Nashville Conference and continued for an additional two years at Cincinnati. This is the fourth annual report, and the last of the present chairman, who has tendered his resignation this week to take up another phase of educational work. Mr. Maddy has been appointed to succeed him, and the new committee will consist of Mr. Maddy, Dr. Rebmann, Mr. Morgan, Mr. Lockhart, and Mr. Fay, with C. M. Tremaine as secretary. The present report summarizes the work of this year along the lines of the Kansas City report of last year."

"A survey of band literature, approved by the Committee and presented in a form similar to that of the orchestra survey of Dr. Rebmann which was included in the report of last year is hereby offered to the Conference. This survey has been made by Mr. Morgan and Mr. Harry Clarke of Cleveland. Acceptance of this report will constitute endorsement of the survey, which will be published by the National Bureau for the Advancement of Music and distributed free in the name of the Committee."

"A standard instrumentation of the Symphonic Band has been published under the auspices of the Committee in a booklet by Mr. Maddy, entitled *School Bands,* issued by the National Bureau. This standard has been approved by Sousa, Goldman, Damrosch and others, and I recommend its endorsement by the Conference. In the same booklet the

Committee sets the standard for smaller bands of various sizes."

"In the matter of publicity the Committee has continued the Instrumental Department in the *Supervisors' Journal*, and the individual members have contributed extensively to other periodicals as they agreed last year. During the year the Committee has published through the National Bureau Mr. Maddy's pamphlet on *School Bands*, a pamphlet by the chairman on *Instrumental Music in the Schools of Rochester and Louisville*, both for free distribution. Mr. Maddy in collaboration with Mr. Giddings has issued a new work on *Orchestral Technique*, that fills a long felt want. The National Bureau will shortly publish a booklet on *School Orchestras*, and one on *Piano Classes*, both calculated to stir up interest in the subject and answer questions of detail and organization. I have a record of at least thirty major articles of practical value on instrumental topics that have been contributed by members of the Committee to the music periodicals during the last four years. I recommend that a future committee publish a list of these and other articles on the subject in periodical literature as a sort of Poole's *Index* for the use of supervisors and training classes. Mr. Tremaine as the Secretary of the Committee has promised that the National Bureau will take care of the publication and distribution of such a list."

"In organization it is hoped that the new Sectional Conferences will adopt the idea of interlocking committees described in last year's report, and that the presence of one instrumental member on each of the state advisory boards will continue to function even better than this year."

"The National Band Contest promoted by the Committee in co-operation with the National Bureau has made astonishing progress in the number of bands competing, in the number of states having contests, and in the quality of the playing. This year a National Contest will be held. A National Band Association has been formed with the Committee acting as a temporary Board of Directors until details of organization shall have been perfected."

"The Committee has been working on a course of instrumental study which it will present in due time."

Instrumental work in all its various forms has created a heavy demand for instructional material which has been met by the issuing of a large number of methods for orchestral instruments. This has been parallelled by large amounts of well edited music for orchestras and bands in all stages of development. Splendid arrangements of the standard classics have been published, the value of which to the orchestra director is doubled by the issuing also of a conductor's score with each number. Valuable treatises dealing with the subject have been published, such as Glenn Woods' *School Orchestras and Bands*, Raymond N.

Carr's *Building the School Orchestra,* and *Instrumental Technique for Orchestra and Band,* by J. E. Maddy and T. P. Giddings.

A similar development of piano class instruction began about 1913 in a few high schools such as those of Cincinnati, but it soon made its way into the grade schools and there evolved a special technique. From ten to twenty pupils or even more have been taught in one class. The paraphernalia for piano-class teaching consists of one or two pianos with two pupils playing at each in turn, and a piano keyboard for each pupil placed before him at his desk or table. Modern methods of teaching music reading have been drawn upon to a large extent. Simple songs which the children have learned to sing are transferred directly to the keyboard. The constant use of applied ear training has produced remarkable results in the ability of the pupils to transpose their music to any key. Several courses of instruction based upon piano arrangements of school songs have been published, and their use has not only resulted in thousands of children learning the piano who would never otherwise have learned, but has given rise to the conviction that class methods for teaching beginners, when skillfully used, have peculiar advantages for the public schools and even for the private studio.

The logic of public school piano instruction from the economic point of view was forcibly stated by Charles H. Miller of Rochester in *School Music* of January, 1924, as follows;—"There is another phase of instrumental work which is very important— probably as much so as the orchestral work—and that is piano class instruction. It is a recent development, having its beginnings in public schools about six years ago. Two years ago a survey of music was made in our schools and we learned that one-fourth of all our children above the third grade were taking piano lessons from private teachers. They were paying on an average about two dollars an hour for each lesson. If we counted thirty-six weeks' instruction, it would amount to $72.00 a year, which is more money than it costs to give a child a year's schooling in all other subjects. Ten thousand of these parents are paying $720,000 a year for private instruction. If that money could be turned over to the music supervisor to use in class instruction, every one of the 48,000 pupils in our schools, including first, second and third grades and kindergarten could be given one class lesson in piano each week, and the majority of the children who are taking private lessons now would progress more rapidly than they do under private instruction. After paying for all this instruction at the rate of $2.50 per hour, we should still have left $288,000 which would be enough to put a $4500 Duo-Art, Steinway, or a Knabe-Grand Ampico in every one of our fifty schools and still have $63,000 left that we would not know what to do with. This great waste is going on every year.

Instruction in piano classes is developing and improving every year, and it has proved so successful in several cities that it has passed the experimental stage. Minneapolis, Lincoln, Nebraska and Pittsburgh have done notable work. Rochester has over 600 in the piano classes, and we are just beginning. While our orchestral department contains only about 1500 students, about 25,000 of our children have pianos in their homes, and practically all their parents are willing and able to pay 25 cents a week for instruction. What would it mean to our city, to our schools, if all these children were trained to play the piano! Here is a means for making a city musical that is within the power of any supervisor to use if she has the determination, the initiative and the will to organize. It need not cost the city anything. The classes can be taught before and after school and at noons, so as not to take any school time, or part of the work can be done on Saturdays. Piano instruction in classes is not so much of an innovation as most people think. The Faelton Music School in Boston is one of the great music schools in this country. They have about 800 students. For the past fifteen years they have been giving the first three years' instruction in classes of twelve. Most of you have heard of the "Fletcher" and "Dunning" methods. The teachers of these systems instruct from four to seven pupils in one group. These systems have been in use for many years."

"The whole problem of music education in the public schools depends upon the success of class instruction.   Private instruction is so expensive that it cannot be considered for a moment in connection with public schools.   We do not make the claim that artists can be produced in the public schools by class instruction; but we do claim that pupils can be so prepared for advanced instruction that only a comparatively short time will be needed for completing an artist's course if the student is of artist caliber."

Educational interest in the piano from the public school viewpoint started with the problems raised by crediting outside study with private teachers.   Three courses have been published which offer carefully graded material designed to answer these problems. These are *The Progressive Series of Piano Lessons*, published by The Art Publication Society, *The Music Students Piano Course*, published by The Oliver Ditson Company, and *The University Course of Music Study*, published by The University Society.

Class piano instruction for the grades has produced a special type of method and material, such as *The Public School Class Method for Piano*, by Giddings and Gilman, *Essentials of Piano Technic*, by Gertrude Kinscella, *Fundamentals of Piano Playing*, by Haake-McConathy, *The Melody Way*, by W. Otto Miessner, and the *Curtis Class Piano System*, by Helen Curtis.

Two different influences have helped to accelerate the nation-wide progress of instrumental instruction. One of these was the junior high school movement which began in the second decade of the century; the other was the World War.

The opportunity offered by the junior high school to adolescent children for the exploration of every field of cultural activity included music in almost every form, and the consequent flexibility of the curriculum allowed boys and girls to find a place in orchestra, band and glee club. The new reorganization of the school system bridged the traditional gulf between the grade and high schools, and made possible a continuous educational growth without a break. The effect upon instrumental music was a continuous chain of ensembles in at least five stages of development, such as grade orchestras, first and second junior, and first and second senior orchestras.

The effect of the World War upon music in the public schools was beyond calculation. We are too near it in point of time to estimate this influence with a true perspective. Two points stand out clearly, however. One is the fundamental importance given to music in winning the war. The value of music was brought home to the people for the time at least with all the force of governmental sanction. Music was shown to be a vital force in national life. Organized singing in the camps and community singing at home became a daily experience. We became, for the time at least, a singing nation welded together by the unifying power of music. The reacting effect educationally was the unqualified acceptance of music as a major subject on the part of both school authorities and the tax payers of the nation.

Another point no less significant was the enormous prestige given to band music. Bands were needed for every training camp and for every regiment. Hundreds of band leaders were trained in government schools. After the war many of these men became instrumental directors in the public schools, and they brought to their task a knowledge of organization and teaching skill of the utmost practical value. Moreover, the military training introduced into the high schools of necessity required a band for every school. The result was an immense acceleration of band activity, accompanied by a new sense of its value as a means of culture and discipline for the youth of the land.

There are no available statistics from which to estimate the progress of instrumental instruction since the war; but we know that now practically every school system large and small has an instrumental department, or provides for such instruction in some form. It is being taught in all teacher training institutions as a part of the preparation of supervisors and special teachers of music. It is making its way steadily into the rural consolidated schools, and the rural county high schools are becoming as well provided for instrumentally as the high schools of the cities.

The evidence of all this is everywhere, and a visit to the high schools of any of our large cities will reveal the almost incredible advance in music education in the past decade. Perhaps as impressive an example as any is that of the Cass Technical High School in Detroit. Beginning in 1919 on a two-hour part time basis, ensemble class work has grown to include 2000 daily lessons given in day and evening classes by a faculty of seventeen music teachers in the day session and fifteen in the evening session. The school articulates with Detroit Teachers College in providing special training for instrumental music teachers. All the music work is on a vocational basis, offering a four year major course in music with the following requirements for graduation, exclusive of courses in English, Mathematics, Economics and Physics;—

First—A study of piano, voice, harmony, musical history and orchestration.

Second—The mastery of at least one orchestra or band instrument; and when possible, learning professionally one string and one wind instrument.

Third—A thorough knowledge of all orchestral and band instruments, acquiring the ability to write for them in different combinations, and at least two years' daily practice in group playing and singing in order to develop the necessary sense of balance and co-ordination.

On the completion of this program of studies the students are prepared to earn a living as professional musicians and have received foundational training necessary for teachers of instruments in class or for conducting bands and orchestras.

The school maintains a full symphony orchestra and symphonic band, concert string quartets, wood wind and harp ensembles, film and dance orchestras, besides other orchestras and bands in progressive stages of maturity.

One of the significant concomitants of post-war instrumental progress is the holding of annual state and regional band contests. It is significant because it implies a long period of careful preparation for the contest, and because it provides one of the best agencies for standardizing school instrumental work. A bulletin issued by the National Bureau for the Advancement of Music shows that in 1925 state band contests were held in Illinois, Indiana, Iowa, Kansas, Michigan, Minnesota, New York, Ohio, South Dakota, Wisconsin, and in addition two mid-west district contests embracing several states each. Also a regional contest was held in Boston. A national contest was held in Chicago in 1923. Of equal import is the growing number of bands and orchestras at the state high school music contests.

Perhaps the crowning indication of school orchestra achievement in the United States was the assembling at the annual meeting of the Music Supervisors National Conference in 1926, of a National High School Orchestra of 246 players from 34 states. Their concert at Orchestra Hall in Detroit, under the leadership of Joseph E. Maddy and Ossip Gabrilovitch was an event of extraordinary importance to the prestige of school-music. To one unfamiliar with the progress of music education in recent years it would have been difficult to believe that the virile and finely balanced performance of the Eroica Symphony was by boys and girls in their teens. A similar orchestra was assembled by Mr. Maddy in March, 1927 for meeting of the Department of Superintendence at Dallas, Texas.

Music Appreciation

The term appreciation, applied to music both in the broad sense of a ruling purpose in school-music and the more restricted sense of a curriculum subject, came into use in the present century. It is conspicuously absent from the discussions and writings of school-music teachers during the preceding epochs. It began to be used at the beginning of the present century to express a broadening conception of what the aim of public school music should be, and about a decade later it became thoroughly identified with studying music by means of listening lessons.

One of the first to outline a course of study in

listening to music was W. S. B. Mathews, whose book *How to Understand Music* came from the press in 1888. This carefully planned work was widely read. It helped to create an interest in the possibilities of this new type of music study. The field for amateur musical study thus invitingly opened was further enriched during the nineties by the interpretive lectures of Walter Damrosch, Thomas W. Surette, Calvin B. Cady and others, as well as by the annotated programs of symphony orchestra concerts, carefully written to make the music more intelligible, and also by the writing of such books as Philip Goepp's *Symphonies and Their Meaning*, Upton's *The Most Famous Oratorios*, and Henderson's *What is Good Music*, all designed to reach the appreciation of the listener by the written and spoken word, as well as by the music itself.

The effectiveness of these helps to the musical understanding of the amateur depended upon some one to play or sing the music which was under consideration, which limited the benefits of such study to a few. But with the epoch making invention of the player-piano and phonograph, and their adaptations to universal use, there soon became available practically the whole of the world's great music. A new era in popular music education began—that of the amateur listener on a nation-wide scale. Player-pianos and phonographs became the possession not only of the homes which already owned a piano, but in large measure of those which did not.

Only gradually and with characteristic caution did the schools make use of these new resources. They did, however, soon begin to use the player-piano for marching the children in and out of the school buildings, and with the perfection of the school type of phonograph it was put to the same use. In some schools, also, attempts were made to use these instruments in the grades for listening to good music, and elective courses in music appreciation making use of them began to be offered in a few high schools. But their wide use for educative purposes had to await the solution of two problems, one, the lack of records especially prepared for school use, the other, an utter inexperience in a method of conducting listening lessons. For these and other reasons, such as the physical difficulties of moving the instruments from room to room, it was not until the second decade of the century that carefully planned lessons in listening to music began to be given and the experience of successful teachers began to be available for general use.

It was in 1911 that the Victor Company organized their educational department and placed Frances E. Clark in charge of the work of making the phonograph a means of real education. Under her leadership the world's music was recorded in suitable form for the school room. Records were made of school song literature, folk songs and dances of all nations, and music discriminative of mood, style and form, and of the tone color and quality of voices and orchestra instruments became available. Other phonograph companies built up similar libraries, and the player-piano companies made records of great piano literature and transcriptions of orchestra music.

Thus there grew up a wealth of recording-instrument material carefully graded from kindergarten through the high school, and this material began to have a wide and ever growing consumption in the schools. Helpful texts for the guidance of the teacher began to be written, such as Anne Shaw Faulkner's *What We Hear in Music* for high schools, and Agnes Fryberger's *Listening Lessons in Music* and Mrs. Clark's *Music Appreciation for Little Children* for the grades. The phonograph companies began to train teachers and send them out into the schools and to teachers' institutes and conventions to show how the subject of appreciation should be taught.

The fifteen years which contain the experience of the schools with listening lessons have seen the phonograph come into common use as an indispensable adjunct of the school room for both appreciation and physical training. At the present time music appreciation with a planned outline of procedure is given in most high schools and in many grade schools. Within the last decade recording pianos such as the Duo-Art and the Ampico have entirely displaced the old type of player-piano, and with their wonderful recordings of the playing of master pianists they are used by an increasing number of schools.

A number of well planned courses for elementary grades have recently been edited and published, all having the purpose of providing a definite place for listening lessons in the regular school program. These have all profited by the accumulated experience of many teachers, and their use will stimulate music educators in further study of the field of appreciation.

These include such books as *Music Appreciation Taught by Means of the Phonograph*, by Kathryn E. Stone, *Reading Lessons in Music Appreciation*, by Mabelle Glenn and Edith M. Rhetts, *Music Appreciation for Every Child*, by Mabelle Glenn, Margaret De Forest and Margaret Lowry, and *Music Appreciation in the School Room*, by Thaddeus P. Giddings, Will Earhart, Ralph L. Baldwin and Elbridge W. Newton.

The main inquiry remains what it was from the beginning—what is the relation of appreciation to school music education? Is it a body of knowledge or an attitude of mind? If appreciation may be defined as a more or less discriminating pleasure in music it is certainly both. There are widely con-

flicting opinions regarding the place of listening lessons in the school.　Some supervisors believe they
should occupy most of the music time in the primary
grades; others that they should be made distinctly
secondary.　The latter cling tenaciously to the idea
that true appreciation comes from actual participation in the music, through singing or playing from
the printed notation.　Nearly everyone believes that
listening lessons can be made a motivating force in
the study of music, whatever form the study takes.
All, however, are agreed that children should have
as much opportunity as possible to hear good music,
and many believe that this is about all that is funda-
mentally important from the listening standpoint.

But however cautiously music supervisors have
moved forward in the matter of formal listening
lessons, they have had no hesitency in making use of
the unique project known as the music memory contest.　The first contest was held in 1916 in the schools
of Westfield, New Jersey, under the supervision of
Mabel Bray.　The subject was brought to the attention of the school music profession by C. M.
Tremaine, director of the National Bureau for the
Advancement of Music in an address before the Music
Supervisors National Conference in 1918.　The response came swiftly.　Within five years it had swept
over the entire country.　The National Bureau
reported in 1926 that it had been introduced into
1083 cities, very many of which have held contests

several years in succession.   In 109 counties it has been conducted on a county-wide scale.   In four states it has been conducted under the auspices of the state educational department.

No single project has received more hearty endorsement than has been given the music memory contest on the part of school music teachers.   While a final evaluation of its educational merits has yet to be made, the experience of supervisors seems to indicate unmistakably that it vitalizes music study, increases ability to work, promotes concentration, observation and memory, and brings to the acquaintance of practically every child a wide range of good music.   A list of one hundred selections most frequently used in three hundred and fifty contests shows that these selections include music from the programs of standard symphony concerts, and of recitals of representative pianists, violinists and singers.

The music memory contest has the distinctive merit, when well administered, of enlisting the participation of a greater number of persons, including children and parents, than any project promoted by the public schools.   A large part of its value lies in its wide community appeal, which brings the school and the home together in a single musical interest. The competitive factor is both a strength and a weakness, but experience has shown that its detrimental features can be minimized by a wise direction of attention to an appreciation of the music.

As acquaintance with music becomes general with the multiplying opportunities of hearing it performed, the memory contest may gradually disappear, or it may contain progressively more exacting factors for competition. So long, however, as a knowledge of standard musical literature remains the possession of comparatively few, the project will contain the same promotive reasons for use which first brought it into favor.

During the last quarter of the nineteenth century the average professional musician thought of public school music with something very much like disdain and contempt. He did not understand the problems of teaching music in the public schools and the results were often of a kind to warrant his disparaging attitude. Since that time a great change has taken place. The professional musician and music supervisor have come nearer together in a realization that both are fellow workers in the field of music, and moreover, the results of school music are increasingly such as compel his respect. One of the finest evidences of this change is the co-operation which began about a decade ago between symphony conductors and music supervisors in arranging programs to be performed especially for children. The selections to be played at these concerts are previously studied in the schools, and at the performance are explained by the director of the orchestra. Such opportunities are enjoyed by the children in New

York (Walter Damrosch was the first to arrange such concerts), Chicago, Detroit, Cleveland, Cincinnati, St. Louis, Kansas City, Minneapolis and other cities which support symphony orchestras. The educational significance of such concerts lies not only in the opportunity of hearing music superbly performed, but also in the fact that they afford a practical basis for appreciation courses planned by expert musicians. Such musical advantages are confined at present to the large cities which have orchestras and the places which they visit on tour, but there is no doubt that the radio will soon bring such music within the reach of all. It is well within the probabilities that not only concerts but formal lessons in appreciation will be regularly broadcasted during school hours as a part of the planned school program. In fact the schools of Connecticut and Massachusetts are already receiving such lessons over the radio. At this writing a plan is being matured by Walter Damrosch to broadcast an extended series of symphony concerts for children.

PROFESSIONAL TRAINING

The steadily increasing breadth and scope of the field of school-music has been parallelled by a corresponding demand for better trained supervisors and special teachers. Before the present century school-music specialists received their training at first from the Boston Academy of Music or from the singing-school conventions which were instituted through the influence of the Academy.   When these institutions came to an end summer schools were organized to make their students familiar with the methods of teaching a particular series of music books.   These summer schools gave excellent training in the three weeks which was their usual duration, but the time was too short to do more than give intensive training in the presentation of material and chorus singing. This preparation sufficed so long as the qualifications of the music supervisor were decided by the individual superintendent and school committee, and music activities were confined to singing and note reading. Moreover, the summer schools did all they could, through enriching their curriculum and through post-graduate courses to give a more thorough preparation to meet the increasing demands of the schools.

During the last twenty-five years, however, the drift of supervisory training has been moving steadily in the direction of normal schools and universities. At the turn of the century nearly all the state normal schools were giving musical training to grade teachers, and with the gradual change of status of these schools to that of college rank, the training of supervisors began to be added.

Early in the century colleges and universities began to establish departments of public school music, connected with their schools of education.   The work offered at their summer sessions enabled teachers in service to apply the credits earned by six weeks of study toward a college degree or license certificate, and as the requirements for certification became increasingly measured in terms of these credits students in great numbers flocked to the university summer schools. The summer music school at Cornell University, directed by Hollis E. Dann, beginning in 1907 was one of the first to offer a six weeks' course with college credit. Between that time and the present hundreds of higher institutions of learning have created school-music departments, and the movement has spread to the conservatories of music, nearly all of which offer training in music supervision and directing. Closely correlated with this music training offered by the colleges was the fact that the states began to regulate the amount of preparation for supervising music, a majority of the states at the present time requiring for certification of music supervisors and special teachers a minimum of two years' work of college grade. In some states the requirements are for a minimum of three years, and the standard all along the line is rising.

In 1923 the Committee on Public School Music of the M. T. N. A. made an inquiry as to the preparation required in the various states for those who teach and supervise music. Their report is contained in the *M. T. N. A. Proceedings* for 1923.

"The average preparation in any state is higher

than the minimum requirement. Not only cities of the first and second class but many smaller individual cities and towns have requirements above the minimum, and will not employ high school teachers who have not a college diploma or its equivalent. Hundreds of students in the music departments of universities and normal schools are taking five, four, and three-year courses, though the minimum average requirement is not more than two years. Many collegiate institutions are offering the degrees of Bachelor of School-Music, Bachelor of Music in Education or Bachelor of Science in Music based upon the four-year course planned by the Educational Council of the Music Supervisors' National Conference. This course, with its harmonious adjustment of academic, pedagogical and musical studies, will, for the time at least, be the standard of efficient preparation for school-music supervising."[1]

In the last two decades of the previous century began the movement to departmentalize instruction which has become a common feature of our schools. The plan at first included the seventh and eighth grades and later was extended to the sixth, and in some systems even to the fifth grade. In recent years some large cities have extended the departmental plan down to the second grade in the form of platoon schools. There seems to be a general tendency toward departmentalizing instruction in as

[1]*M. T. N. A. Proceedings*—1923.

many grades as experience proves practicable.   Obviously, if the platoon idea were adopted by all schools the problem of music instruction would be much simplified.   Every one who taught music would then be a specialist, the number requiring special music training would be much less than at present, and the preparation would be more extensive and exacting, all of which would logically result in a uniformly higher quality of school-music.   At the present time, however, practically all music instruction in the first six grades is in the hands of the grade teachers.

The growing insistence on the part of State Boards of Education upon more and better training for school music teachers made natural and inevitable the appointing of state directors or supervisors of music.   The movement began with Pennsylvania in the appointment of Paul E. Beck in 1917.   Mr. Beck was succeeded by Hollis Dann in 1921, and Dr. Dann by M. Claude Rosenberry in 1925.   Russell Carter, after serving the state department of New York as Specialist in Music in 1921, became state supervisor of music of that state in 1923.   The other states having state music supervisors, with the present incumbents, are: Ohio, Edith M. Keller; Delaware, Glenn Gildersleeve; Louisiana, Samuel T. Burns; Missouri, Lytton S. Davis; Montana, Marguerite V. Hood.

An important influence upon professional training, broadly considered, has been the growing number of valuable books, pamphlets, and articles dealing with various aspects of the work of school-music teaching. The tune-books which were used in the singing-schools and conventions always contained a treatise upon the elements of music and suggestions for teaching them, interspersed with philosophical comments. When courses of school-music books began to appear, beginning with the *National Music Course*, the same kind of suggestions were included either in the books of the course, or in separate teachers' manuals. This kind of writing has had a large influence in establishing principles and standards of teaching.

As early as 1852 another type of writing began with various articles printed in *Dwight's Journal of Music*, which was published in Boston from 1852 to 1882, a total of 40 volumes. These were mainly reportorial in character, and were written by correspondents from different states, or were in the form of letters written by teachers, or critical editorials from the pen of John S. Dwight, the editor of the Journal. Similar articles were printed also in *The Musician*, the immediate successor of *Dwight's Journal*, and in *The Musical Courier*, and in *Music*, edited and published by W. S. B. Mathews for several years beginning about 1890.

The Journal of Education, dating from 1875 (beginning under the title *New England Journal of Education*), from the first issue contained frequent articles by music supervisors. The Tonic Sol-fa versus the Staff controversy between T. F. Seward and H. E. Holt was given space in its columns in the eighties, and its pages increasingly from year to year gave attention to the subject of school music. In the early years of the present century it printed many articles by Robert Foresman dealing with the philosophy of the song method. Dr. A. E. Winship, the editor of the *Journal of Education*, has written many penetrating editorials on the purpose of teaching music in the schools.

From 1885 until 1888 the F. H. Gilson Company of Boston published the *School Music Journal* —a monthly periodical, which served the cause of school music well during its brief existence.

The *Books of Proceedings* of the N. E. A. contained the minutes of the meetings of the Music Section of that body, but up to 1900 few if any addresses were included.

The literature of the school-music profession may be said to really begin with Philip C. Hayden's magazine, *School-Music*, in 1900. The twenty-six volumes of this magazine contain reports of association meetings, addresses, discussions, and scores of special articles, all of which constitute a valuable and permanent record of school-music opinion. Other permanent records of the same character and value are the *Books of Proceedings* of the Music Teachers National Association, published yearly beginning

with 1906, the *Books of Proceedings* of the Music
Supervisors' National Conference, published yearly
since 1912, the *Music Supervisors' Journal*, dating
from 1914, and the *Eastern School Music Herald*,
dating from 1918.

Other important publications of a different type
are the United States Government pamphlets edited
by Will Earhart or by committees of which he was
chairman.   In this class also are the bulletins prepared by the National Research Council of Music
Education and published by the Music Supervisors'
National Conference.   Also should be mentioned the
many pamphlets and books published by the National
Bureau for the Advancement of Music.

Of special value to the growing volume of school-
music literature have been such books as Francis E.
Howard's *The Child Voice in Singing*, John Dawson's
The Voice of the Boy, Thomas Tapper's *The Music
Supervisor*, Frank R. Rix's *Manual of School Music*,
Charles H. Farnsworth's *Education Through Music*,
and *How to Study Music*, Karl W. Gehrkens'
The Essentials of Conducting, *Music Notation and
Terminology*, *An Introduction to School Music
Teaching*, and *Fundamentals of Music*, Cundiff
and Dykema's *School-Music Handbook*, Thaddeus
P. Giddings' *Grade School Music Teaching*, and
Giddings' and Baker's *High School Music Teaching*,
Edwin N. C. Barnes' *Who's Who in Music Education*,
Archibald T. Davison's *Music Education in America*,

and *Tests and Measurements in Music*, by Jacob Kualwasser, besides many books and pamphlets dealing with instrumental work and music-appreciation.

COMMUNITY MUSIC

Public school music sprang from community music. The original singing-school was the community learning together, old and young, the elements of music and the songs which could be used by the same people in the church. The singing-school convention was community music on a larger scale, drawing its singers from near and far, even from beyond the state borders, and spending several days in studying various forms of music which were of community concern, music for the singing-school, the church, the sunday school, the choral society, and in training teachers and leaders. The Boston Convention added the cultivation of children's voices in chorus, and thus helped directly the introduction of music into the Boston schools. Practically all the music of this period, the first half of the nineteenth century, might be classed as community music. Its participants were predominantly amateurs, and the amateur spirit prevaded it all.

In the last third of the century the influence of the Convention waned and finally disappeared and with it disappeared all co-ordination between music in the school, church and choral society. All went their several ways. Professionalism came to the front and created a musical class consciousness, and the typical music student, dreaming of a musical career as concert soloist, drew away from amateur enterprises. The solo church quartet largely displaced the traditional chorus choir. School-music withdrew to the four walls of the school room and began to hunt for a solution of how to teach all the children to read music. In solving this problem it made two priceless discoveries—the beautiful singing tone of children and the individual child himself, with his varying abilities.

Meanwhile the amateur spirit lived on, though in a somewhat subdued way, in choir, choral society and town band, until in the twentieth century it began to take on a new lease of life, making its way into the myriad groups of modern community life. Its manifestations are today everywhere about us—in the church choral society, the Sunday-School choir and orchestra, the Y. M. C. A. orchestra and massed singing, singing in the shops and industries and their use of bands and orchestras, singing in the lodges, the Rotary, Kiwanis and Lions Clubs, in such community enterprises as Christmas tree celebrations, National Music Week, neighborhood carolling, and in pageantry, celebrating town and city anniversaries.

This renaissance of the amateur spirit in music is an expression of democracy. It affords the opportunity and encouragement of each person old and young to use the music that is in him in co-operation with others. Music, like all the fine arts has its aristocracies, but in its community expression it is increasingly democratic.

The amateur enterprise has been sponsored and forwarded by such men as Frank Damrosch in the People's Singing Classes in New York, Samuel W. Cole in the People's Choral Union in Boston, and Harry Barnhart in his community singing leadership. Organizations such as The National Community Music League, The National Bureau for the Advancement of Music, and The National Federation of Music Clubs exist solely for the purpose of encouraging participation in music. The latter is a gigantic community music organization, working to develop musical enterprise throughout the land, articulating with the public schools through its junior music clubs and in efforts for state music supervision, and with the private teacher in offering prizes for excellence in performance, and with the composers in prize awards for compositions of outstanding merit.

The National Bureau for the Advancement of Music was established in 1916 with C. M. Tremaine as executive director. As its name implies the National Bureau uses all its resources in efforts to assist in all forms of musical advancement. The ten years record of its service to the cause of music is an enviable one, and it has gained the universal confidence of musicians and ·music educators. The

Bureau has been of peculiar value to supervisors of music in promoting the music memory contest, in gathering and publishing statistics regarding outside credits for applied music and other forms of school-music work, in acting as headquarters for National Music Week, in promoting band contests, and in its general readiness to act as a clearing house for all community aspects of public school music.

In all types of community participation in music, public school teachers and supervisors have had a share. The central message in Thomas Tapper's book, *The Music Supervisor*—that this individual should embody the spirit of community music—is being lived out in the school-music profession. Specific instances would require a volume in itself. They would include such enterprises as Will Earhart's Community Orchestra and Chorus in Richmond, Indiana, Hollis Dann's Music Festivals at Ithaca, New York, Frank Rix leading the massed singing of thousands in the parks of New York City, Walter Aiken's organizing the kindergarten mothers of Cincinnati into a singing group, Frank A. Beach's extension of the resources of Kansas Teachers College to reach the entire state, Charles A. Fullerton's similar work in Iowa, Edgar B. Gordon's organization of the town of Winfield, Kansas, into a community music enterprise, and Peter W. Dykema's leadership of community singing during the World War. Mr. Dykema's leadership has not been confined to song leading. He has made dozens of addresses dealing with every phase of the rising democracy of music, and his many magazine articles have persistently emphasized the musical possibilities of the ordinary citizen, boy, girl, man and woman. An instance of the union of all the music of a city under one leadership is that of Flint, Michigan, where William W. Norton holds the position of supervisor of music and civic music director, a position formerly held by George Oscar Bowen.

School-music is no longer cloistered. Its spirit is that of co-operation and helpfulness. School and community are rapidly coming together. The spirit which is making America musically powerful today is the same spirit, adapted to changing conditions, of which Lowell Mason was the embodiment.

Chapter VIII

MUSIC TEACHERS' ASSOCIATIONS
THE CONFERENCE MOVEMENT

C LOSELY interrelated and running parallel with public school progress have been the many national, sectional and state teachers' associations, whose activities embrace every general and special professional interest. The oldest of these is the American Institute of Instruction, organized in 1830 in the city of Boston. William C. Woodbridge addressed this body at one of its first sessions in the interest of music as a school subject, thus opening the campaign which resulted in the introduction of music into the Boston schools. This address aroused a good deal of favorable interest in the subject, an interest which was carried into the eleven states represented at the Institute. In 1849 a national convention of teachers was organized, with Horace Mann as president. Later, in 1857 this body developed into the National Education Association, at present the largest body of teachers in the world.

The first national assemblage of teachers organized exclusively in the interest of music was The

National Music Congress which met at Boston in 1869. This congress was brought together through the initiative of Eben Tourjee, head of the New England Conservatory of Music, who stated that its object was "to arrive at a greater unity of purpose and of method in the musical development of the American people." The impulse which brought about this convention came from the effect upon hundreds of music teachers of the World's Peace Jubilee held in Boston in July, 1869. The great festival chorus of 10,000 voices was recruited from choirs, singing societies and singing-schools from the New England and other states. Many of the leaders of these organizations discovered that they had common interests which could be strengthened by an organization. A second meeting of the Congress was held in New York in 1870 and a third in Boston in 1871. At this session Governor Claflin, of Massachusetts said, "It was one of the happy results of the great Peace Jubilee that the whole standard of music was raised higher; that the whole people learned from it the necessity of more thorough instruction in the art. The result was seen in the action of the last legislature of this state, which, though it failed to pass a law by which the larger cities and towns should make instruction in music compulsory, to be paid for by the municipalities, yet it developed so much feeling in favor of such action that for my part I can hardly expect another session to pass by

without the law taking its place in the statute books."
The secretary of the Congress reported that the
"labors of the congress have been productive of good
results, both of its primary objects—the formation
and development of choral societies and the promotion
of the teaching of music in the public schools of the
land—have been very successful."[1]

This pioneer organization did not survive its
third meeting. The movement thus initiated bore
permanent fruit, however, in the Music Teachers
National Association, which had its first meeting at
Delaware, Ohio, Dec. 27, 1876, with Eben Tourjee
as president. Its object was to raise the professional
standards of music teaching. The meetings at first
were general sessions, and all addresses and discussions took place before the entire membership. The
association regarded all the phases of music education
as forming one general problem, of interest to all
teachers, and this attitude made the M. T. N. A. a
broadening and uniting influence in the music teaching profession. School-music teachers were given
plenty of opportunity to be heard, and men like L.
W. Mason, N. Coe Stewart, H. W. Fairbank and T.
F. Seward ably presented the subject at its meetings
in the early years.

At this period the old-time six-weeks normal
music institutes were beginning to change over into
permanent music schools, and with the rapid increase

[1] *Dwight's Journal of Music*—July 1, 1871.

everywhere in the number of private music teachers, the M. T. N. A. became naturally the representative body of this profession.   Two annual meetings only have been omitted since its organization in 1876. Various phases of its work were gradually handed over to standing committees, including among others one on public school music, and since 1906 all records of its meetings together with reports of committees and prepared addresses have been published annually in a *Book of Proceedings*.

The several public school committees of the Association have done good work in clarifying the aims of school-music and in raising its standards.   At the time when music was struggling for credit recognition in high schools it helped to make clear the justice of the situation, and in 1907 and '08 under the chairmanship of Ralph Baldwin the committee prepared the first professional statement of the results which should be expected from music in the elementary grades.   Various valuable surveys have been made also by the several committees.   The work of the Music Teachers National Association was considerably expanded during the last quarter of the nineteenth century by the formation of many state music teachers associations, organized along the same lines as the National.

In July, 1884, the same year in which Hosea E. Holt opened his Lexington summer school, a number of public school music teachers met at Madison, Wisconsin, at the time of the annual meeting of the N. E. A. This meeting was brought about through the efforts of Luther Whiting Mason and Theodore F. Seward. It was voted to petition the board of directors of the National Association for admission as a department of the Association. The petition was granted and the department of public school-music was organized. For several years the meetings were mainly given up to discussion as to how public school-music might be extended, and to spirited debates as to the relative merits of the Tonic Sol-fa and the Staff systems of notation, there being at this time a rather determined effort to spread the teaching of Tonic Sol-fa in this country. Theodore F. Seward championed the Tonic Sol-fa and Hosea E. Holt the staff. In 1892 the department passed what seems to have been the first resolution ever framed by a professional school-music body regarding the aims of school music, as follows;—

"Resolved;—that it is the sense of the music section—

"1st—that sight-singing, that is, the thinking of musical tones in their scale and harmonic relations, the thinking of rhythm, of tone length, and the quick perception of the signs which stand for these definite mental concepts, should be taught, in the primary grades and made the basis of all work in music;

"2nd—that good quality of tone should be taught in all exercises and songs; and the voices of children should be protected from injury by avoiding the extremes of high and low pitch, or of loud and soft singing, and by securing distinct articulation;

"3rd—that correct intonation and blended voices in part singing should be developed.

"4th—that musical taste should be cultivated by the use of the best music in all grades;

"5th—that emotional or expressive singing should be secured."[1]

Beginning with 1893 the meetings showed decided restlessness regarding some of the current practices in teaching music. A discussion of the topic "Learning to Read Musical Notation" showed the beginning of a protest against starting notation too early. The topic "Harmony in Music" revealed wide difference of opinion as to the grade for beginning alto singing, varying from the first grade to the fifth. There was also discussed the question of "The danger of confining the course of study too long to singing mechanical exercises devoid of artistic merit and empty of all thought and feeling."[2]

Toward the close of the decade the Music Section of the N. E. A. began to take on the character of national leadership in school music and the meetings became constructively valuable and were largely attended. At the meeting in Charleston, S. C., in 1900, Sterrie A. Weaver made a strong plea for in-

[1] *N. E. A. Proceedings,* Music Section, 1892.
[2] *N. E. A. Proceedings,* Music Section, 1893.

dividual singing, declaring that more than seventy-five per cent of the children could be taught to sing individually, whereas not more than twenty-five per-cent could sing individually by the methods commonly taught.   At the same meeting C. H. Congdon explained the philosophy of the song-method, which was coming to the front at this time.

It is necessary to interrupt the narrative at this point for a consideration of some other phases of the music convention movement.

The formation of the National Education Association had been followed by similar types of organizations in the various states, taking the form of state, district or county teachers associations, and after the formation of the Music Section of the N. E. A. similar sections were formed in the smaller associations.

The national associations reached only a small proportion of the rank and file of those engaged in school-music work.   Of far more influence upon the thought and method of the small town supervisor and music teacher were the state and district associations, and the summer music schools which were attended by hundreds of teachers.   Toward the end of the century such organizations as the Music Sections of the Central and Southern Illinois, the Southeastern Iowa and many others in widely scattered parts of the country became more and more active in bringing school-music teachers together.   The district association movement was becoming general throughout the country, and there was little difference discernable between the national and sectional groups in the range of topics brought forward for discussion, such as the song-method, the scale-method, the child voice, the teaching of rhythm and the growing importance of high school music.

All of the groups of school-music teachers thus far mentioned were adjuncts or departments of national or state associations. The movement to form independent bodies of school-music teachers did not commence until near the end of the century, though as early as 1885 a meeting of music teachers at Pilgrim Hall, Boston, resolved itself into an organization with the title "The New England Public School Music Teachers Association." In 1897, at the meeting of the music section of the N. E. A., at Milwaukee, upon the motion of Philip C. Hayden an organization came into being under the name "The National Federation of School Music Teachers," the first school-music association to bear the name "National." The sole function of this body was to share in the distribution of full printed reports of the meetings of the music section of the N. E. A. The National Federation was thus merely a mailing list, but it indicated the feeling of need for wider dissemination of professional opinion among the music teachers of the country, only a small number of whom could attend the national meetings. The

National Federation flourished for three years and then ceased operations, its aims having meanwhile been provided for in the *School Music Monthly*, which Philip C. Hayden began publishing in 1900.

In July, 1899, at Utica, N. Y., "The Society of American School Music Supervisors" was organized with Sterrie A. Weaver, president, Julia Ettie Crane, vice-president, T. L. Roberts, treasurer, Ralph L. Baldwin, secretary, and J. H. Humphrey, auditor. This society had a short but vigorous existence.   It survived two meetings, the second of which was held at New Haven, Connecticut in 1900, and which was characterized by a determination to put into practice the spirit of its articles of association, which stated that "The sole object of this association shall be the advancement of school music teaching, an honest search for the truth and a determination to appropriate the ways, means and methods which prove to give the best results, and this without regard to the brand, name or guise in which they are discovered. We call upon all members of the profession throughout the country to aid in honest, fearless discussion of the subject, believing that the elevation of music in all the schools to its rightful place will result only from a united effort.   It is not the purpose of this association to conflict with any state or national music organization."   This was the most spirited statement regarding its aims ever framed by a body of school-music teachers, and the energy of the leaders of the ephemeral "Society of American School Music Supervisors" was carried over into the work of the other existing associations.

Certainly this sort of constructive energy was displayed by the Music Section of the N. E. A. beginning with 1900 and thereafter, noticeable especially in its disposition to work through committees.

The meeting at Minneapolis in 1902 developed a strong purpose to raise the standards of school-music teaching. Thomas Tapper and Hollis Dann read papers dealing with the unsatisfactory status of music in the public schools owing to poor preparation on the part of supervisors and grade teachers. A committee was appointed consisting of Thomas Tapper, A. J. Gantvoort and Oscar T. Corson, later increased by two others, to formulate a course of study for teachers of music in the public schools, the first action to be thus taken regarding supervisory preparation.

The Boston meeting in 1903 was one of the strongest ever held by the Department. The notable demonstration of sight-reading under the direction of Sterrie A. Weaver occurred at this meeting. A resolution was passed to the effect that it is a wrong method to teach the details of musical notation below the third grade. A committee of ten was appointed to formulate a statement of results to be expected of grade work, with the following members;—Sterrie A. Weaver, Anna M. Allen, Estelle Carpenter, A.

J. Gantvoort, Julia Ettie Crane, B. C. Davis, Edward
B. Birge, Francis E. Howard, H. M. Butler and C.
A. Fullerton.

At the meeting at St. Louis, in 1904, the report
of the New England Education League on a high
school course of study in music was presented and
was adopted. This was the first formulation of a
high school music course to be adopted by a body of
school-music teachers. The committee of five made
a partial report on the preparation of the music
teacher, and the committee of ten a partial report on
results to be expected from grade work.

At Asbury Park, New Jersey, in 1905, the
report of the committee of five on the training of the
supervisor, headed by Thomas Tapper was adopted.
It recommended literary qualifications equal at least
to that of a high school graduate, and musical qualifications to include proficiency on some instrument and
the ability to sing, and in addition a practical knowledge of theory, history of music, conducting, and a
bibliography of school-music books, including courses
of study. The report included also recommendations
regarding the examination for music supervisors and
suggestions as to the musical requirements of grade
teachers. This report, though ineffective from lack
of machinery for carrying out its suggestions, was
valuable as suggesting positive standards for training schools, and was noteworthy as being the first
statement of supervisory training to be officially

approved by the then most representative body of supervisors in the United States.

The meeting scheduled for San Francisco in 1906, had to be abandoned, on account of the great catastrophe of earthquake and fire which occurred in the spring of that year.

In 1906, a committee was appointed by Hamlin E. Cogswell, president of the Music Section of the N. E. A., to inquire into the subject of needed changes in the terminology of music. The members of this committee were Charles I. Rice, Constance B. Smith, Leo R. Lewis, William B. Kinnear and Philip C. Hayden. This committee submitted a report at every meeting of the N. E. A. between 1907 and 1914, securing the adoption of the precise meanings of more than thirty commonly used musical terms. They carried on an extensive correspondence with each other and with teachers and musicians in all parts of the country. Their labors, which covered a period of seven years, called forth a good deal of controversial writing, which, together with the findings of the committee appeared in the columns of *School Music*. The committee performed one of the most satisfactory pieces of work ever done in the service of school-music.

At the meeting of the music section of the N. E. A. at Los Angeles in 1907, Hamlin E. Cogswell, Elsie M. Shawe and Estelle Carpenter were appointed a committee on a uniform version of patriotic songs. As this committee was not ready with a report at the

1908 meeting at Cleveland, another committee consisting of A. J. Gantvoort, Elsie M. Shawe and Osbourne McConathy was appointed to confer with musicians and teachers throughout the country in regard to their views upon the selection and musical arrangement of the national songs.

At Denver, in 1909, the committee, not being able to agree upon a version of the four patriotic songs chosen, *(Hail Columbia, Columbia the Gem of the Ocean, America* and *The Star Spangled Banner)*, a committee of ten was appointed to give the matter further consideration, consisting of A. J. Gantvoort, Osbourne McConathy, Elsie M. Shawe, Rossiter W. Cole, Thomas Tapper, C. H. Farnsworth, Edward B. Birge, Frances E. Clark, Jessie L. Gaynor and Mrs. C. B. Kelsey. At Boston in 1910, the committee's report with respect to the melodies only was adopted and the committee continued for another year. At San Francisco in 1911, the committee's version of *The Star Spangled Banner* and *Hail Columbia* was criticised and referred back to the committee for further consideration. Finally, at Chicago in 1912, the report on national songs was adopted and the committee dismissed. The question of the national songs was reopened by the entrance of the United States into the World War, and disposed of by the committee on community song-book of the Music Supervisors National Conference, consisting of Peter W. Dykema, Hollis Dann, Osbourne McConathy and Will Earhart.

The period of greatest influence of the Music Section of the N. E. A. was during the first decade of the twentieth century. In these ten years attendance at the meetings was very large and the Department grew strong in leadership. It became accustomed to working through committees and to making plans and policies which implied a sense of solidarity and continuance. The Department became in effect a national body of music supervisors. The resulting consciousness of the power in united effort brought about a desire on the part of many leading supervisors for an independent national association. The opportunity was not long in coming.

THE CONFERENCE MOVEMENT

In January, 1905, Philip C. Hayden began publishing a series of articles giving an exposition of his method of teaching the tonal side of music through a progressive series of rhythm forms to which he gave the general title, *Ear Training in Rhythm Forms*. These articles and the editorial comments which followed them almost uninterruptedly for two years called wide attention to Mr. Hayden's music teaching in the schools of Keokuk, Iowa. During the last week in November, 1906, Mr. Hayden sent the following letter to about thirty supervisors in the middle west:

"Dear sir,—This is the fourth year I have been basing all my work in school-music on rhythm.   During the last years I have completed a method of practicing these 'rhythm forms.'   The application of foundation principles which I make in classifying the elements of music is so original, the method used in training the ear to recognize the different rhythm groups so new, and the results of this new method are so entirely satisfactory that I am extremely anxious to have the work inspected by a large group of supervisors."

"I would like to have a body of supervisors come here at the same time and investigate the work I am doing.   Would it not be possible at such a time to have a convention of the supervisors of the middle west to last, say two days, comprising six lessons with a regular program, my work on ear training in rhythm forms to take up two or three of these sessions, the rest of the meeting to be given up to problems of general interest, to papers and discussions?"

"If I could get a dozen or fifteen representative supervisors to come to Keokuk, would you be willing to come, if nothing special interfered with your leaving home at the time agreed upon?"

This letter shows that the proposed conference was not to be a national affair.   Evidently Mr. Hayden had no thought of supervisors from the east or far west being able to attend owing to the great distances to be traveled.

As a result of the hearty response which the letter brought forth, a call was published in *School Music* of January, 1907, signed by twenty-six music supervisors, and reading as follows;—

"It being almost certain that the annual meeting of the N. E. A. will be held in the extreme east or extreme west next summer, it seems desirable to hold a meeting of school-music supervisors in the middle west. Believing in the value of such a conference, and fully intending to be present ourselves, the undersigned hereby call for a gathering of supervisors of school-music, to come together at Keokuk, Iowa, at some date to be settled later. The official board of the N. E. A. will be asked to appoint a committee to arrange a program for this conference."

The list of signers was headed by the names of the three board members referred to, namely, Hamlin E. Cogswell, Mrs. Frances E. Clark and P. C. Hayden.

Such were the preliminary happenings which led to the gathering of the first music-supervisors' conference, an event which, though apparently unimportant at the time, marks one of the mile-stones of school-music history. For this gathering was the nucleus of the Music Supervisors' National Conference, an organization which, with its allied conferences has become the most important factor in the twentieth century progress of school-music.

Of the 104 persons who attended the Keokuk
Conference, April 10-12, 1907, sixty-nine became
permanent members.   Sixteen states were represented.   Owing to the illness of Hamlin E. Cogswell,
who had been scheduled to preside, Frances E. Clark
became chairman of the meetings.   The conference
was held in the Westminister Presbyterian Church,
with three sessions each of the three days.   The
meetings were very informal, and with the exception
of the demonstration of Mr. Hayden's school work,
and Jessie Gaynor's Operetta *The House that Jack
Built*, presented under the direction of Hortense
Reynolds, supervisor of music of Des Moines, Iowa,
the program as previously planned underwent considerable rearrangement.   There were few set speeches
or prepared papers; but there was a very liberal
amount of discussion and a marked spirit of comrade-
ship.   It was evident that the supervisors present
had come together partly at least because of the
novelty of meeting as an independent body of school-
music teachers.

The major topic, of course, was the consideration of rhythm-forms as used by Mr. Hayden in the
Keokuk schools, and which were demonstrated by
groups of children from the various grades.   As
showing the ability of the pupils to sing many
varieties of scale and interval groups in the seven
rhythm-forms the demonstration was a success; but
when they attempted to apply this ability to reading

new music the results were not conclusive. Some of the classes read with confidence, and some failed, partly from nervousness. It was evident that the children had been well drilled on the rhythm-forms, but that practice in reading actual music had received scant attention, and perhaps had been purposely neglected, because Mr. Hayden was honestly trying to prove that a good working knowledge of rhythm-forms involving the ordinary melodic idioms of music would enable the child to successfully attack the printed page. However, the demonstration presented the reading problem in a somewhat new aspect, which gave an opportunity for this ever old and ever new question to be analyzed.

Several other topics came before the conference. Alys E. Bentley, of Washington, D. C., and T. P. Giddings of Oak Park, Illinois, presented the question of the child's use of the voice. C. A. Fullerton spoke on the subject "How Can We Develop Skill in Sight Reading Without Sacrificing Musical Spirit?" The other topics discussed were Terminology and Authorized Versions of National Songs. Hortense Reynolds, of Des Moines, Iowa, conducted a performance of Jessie Gaynor's operetta, *The House that Jack Built.*

The demand for a uniform terminology grew out of the careless use of musical terms on the part of music teachers. As discussions of the details of methodology at convention meetings and in magazine articles necessitated the constant use of such terms, it became more and more imperative that all should use the same term for the same thing. Moreover, a wide variation had grown up in class-room teaching in the use of such terms as note, tone, rhythm, measure, bar, meter, beat, natural, cancel, chromatic and accidental, all tending toward mental confusion and emphasizing the need of a uniform and consistent use of musical terminology. Hence the agitation for terminology reform.

The importance of teaching our national songs in the public schools had become universally recognized, and this led to a desire, more and more insistent on the part of music teachers for a uniform and standard version of these songs.

At the first session of the Keokuk Conference there was no idea in the minds of the members to make the organization a permanent one. The music section of the N. E. A. was regarded as the national representative organization of school-music teachers, and it had all the prestige which went with a continuous active existence extending through a period of over twenty years. But by the end of the second day considerable sentiment began to be expressed in favor of making the conference a permanent, independent body. This led to the appointment of an organization committee with Herman E. Owen as chairman, who at the final session brought in a report making the conference a permanent organization.

The report was adopted and the following officers were elected;—President, Philip C. Hayden, Vice-president, Charles H. Miller, secretary, Stella R. Root, treasurer, Edward B. Birge. The executive committee in addition to the foregoing, were Frances E. Clark, T. P. Giddings, Herman E. Owen and Birdie Alexander.

No name was chosen for the new organization, though it was commonly known as "The Music Supervisors Conference."

In an editorial in the May, 1907, number of *School Music*, P. C. Hayden wrote as follows regarding the name;—"In regard to the extent of the Music Supervisors Conference and the name which should wisely be chosen, two opinions were expressed. One was that it would be an assumption on the part of the supervisors present at this meeting to call the organization a National Supervisors Conference. A second opinion expressed was that no name should be chosen which limited the membership to any particular section; that the organization and name should be such that all supervisors in this country should feel that the organization was open to them. The writer suggests that adopting the simple name Music Supervisors Conference would meet the objections set forth in these two opinions. The name Music Supervisors Conference neither limits the territory nor claims national significance."

There was no meeting of the new organization

during 1908, owing to the fact that the N. E. A. met that year at Cleveland, which was geographically accessible to a majority of the members. There was the psychological reason also of long allegiance and loyalty to the N. E. A.

In 1909, the Conference met at Indianapolis, with about 100 in attendance. The chief discussion at this meeting centered in the report upon grammar-grade requirements of music teaching, as presented at the Washington meeting of the Music Teachers National Association the previous year by Ralph L. Baldwin, chairman of the public school committee of that body.

In 1910, the Conference met at Cincinnati, with a membership of about 150. It was at this meeting that the name "The Music Supervisors National Conference" was adopted by the organization together with a constitution. One day was spent in visiting schools, a practice which each successive meeting has followed. The Conference began constructive work on a high school music course through a committee consisting of Will Earhart, Hollis Dann, Walter Aiken, E. B. Birge and Karl W. Gehrkens. Elsie M. Shawe, of St. Paul, Minnesota, presented a composite paper on "Standardization of Sight Reading," representing the opinions of a committee of ten previously appointed.

In 1911, the Conference met at Detroit. At

this meeting the committee on high school music submitted a preliminary report.

At the meeting in 1912, at St. Louis, Dr. Carl Seashore of Iowa State University presented the subject "Measurement of Musical Talent" for the first time before the Conference. A report presented by the high school committee contained the important principle that all work in music should receive credit on the basis of either prepared lessons or as laboratory work.

In 1913, at the Rochester meeting the subject of high school orchestras was stressed for the first time. A committee on making a selection of songs for community singing was appointed, headed by Peter W. Dykema.

At the meeting in 1914, at Minneapolis, efficiency in music teaching was the central topic. Will Earhart gave a preliminary report of the music committee of the Commission on the Reorganization of Secondary Education. The question of the Conference undertaking the issue of a quarterly bulletin was also first tentatively discussed at this meeting.

In 1915, at the Pittsburgh meeting the membership reached 350. At this meeting the subject of community singing was stressed and the Conference started the custom of informal singing under leadership which has been a feature of all subsequent meetings.

Peter W. Dykema, the editor of the *Music*

Supervisors' Bulletin, the new official organ of the Conference, reported that four issues had been printed, with a total of 25,000 copies, sent out in four quarterly installments. At the request of the Conference, Karl W. Gehrkens submitted a statement of the consensus of opinion as to the aims of school-music as follows;—

"The ultimate aim of music teaching in the public schools is to cause children to know, to love and to appreciate music in as many forms as possible, and thus to bring added joy into their lives and added culture and refinement into their natures."

"The specific means for accomplishing these aims may vary considerably in various places, but it is the sense of this body of music supervisors that the most direct approach is at present to be found in the expressive singing by the children themselves of a large amount of the best music available, and it is their belief that in this singing the art side and the science side of music need not necessarily be antagonistic, as some have seemed to assume, but may each contribute something to the sum total of musical influence that we are seeking to exert upon the child. It is our belief, also, however, that when the science side is emphasized, it should always be as a means to an end and never as an end in itself. In other words, that although skill in sight-singing, keenness in analysis in ear training, and some knowledge of theoretical facts may all be desirable, yet these technical aspects of musical study must never be allowed to interfere with the legitimate working out of those emotional and aesthetic phases of music which constitute the real essence of the art; in other words, that it is the art side of music with its somewhat intangible influence which we are seeking to cultivate rather than the science side with its possibilities along the line of mental training and its more easily classified results."

In 1916, the Conference met at Lincoln, Nebraska. At this meeting a choral concert was given by the whole membership under the leadership of William L. Tomlins. Thereafter the choral concert became a regular part of the annual program. For the first time, also, there was a discussion and demonstration of violin class-teaching before the Conference.

The meeting at Grand Rapids, in 1917, emphasized instrumental work and a full demonstration was given of class violin playing by a large group of children. The annual choral concert was divided into two parts, the first being community singing led by Harry H. Barnhart, and the second a program by the conference chorus directed by Father W. J. Finn. The community singing feature was retained in subsequent annual concerts. An important feature of this meeting was the first breaking away from exclusively general meetings and apportioning to round tables the problems arising from the growing expansion of school music.

In 1918, at the meeting at Evansville, Indiana, the entrance of the nation into the World War gave a strong tone of patriotism to the sessions. John Alden Carpenter gave an address on "Music in the Camps." At this meeting the Conference took one of the most important steps in its history in electing an Educational Council of ten members, whose duties were to make a thorough study of the problems of school music, and report annually to the Conference. The Council thus elected consisted of Will Earhart, Karl W. Gehrkens, Hollis Dann, Peter W. Dykema, Charles H. Farnsworth, Thaddeus P. Giddings, Alice C. Inskeep, Osbourne McConathy, W. Otto Miessner, and Charles H. Miller.

At the meeting in 1919, at St. Louis, Osbourne McConathy in his presidential address gave the first formulation of what may be considered the present governing principle of public school music as follows;—"Every child should be educated in music according to his natural capacities, at public expense, and his studies should function in the musical life of the community."

The first report of the Educational Council was presented by the chairman, Will Earhart. Peter W. Dykema, editor of the *Music Supervisors Journal*, (the new name for the original Bulletin) reported that the circulation had reached the 9000 mark, and

First Educational Council
Music Supervisors' National Conference

WILL EARHART

KARL W. GEHRKENS

OSBOURNE McCONATHY

PETER W. DYKEMA

HOLLIS E. DANN

THADDEUS P. GIDDINGS

CHARLES H. FARNSWORTH

ALICE C. INNSKEEP

W. OTTO MIESSNER

CHARLES H. MILLER

that it "has been sent free to all individuals who are known to be associated with public school music teaching and to all others who had indicated that they were interested in it." Mr. Dykema also made a report for the committee on "Community Song Book" giving its evolution from the original pamphlet, *Eighteen Songs for Community Singing*, issued in 1913, to the enlarged booklet, *Fifty-five Songs for Community Singing*, which was compiled by Hollis Dann, Will Earhart, Osbourne McConathy and Peter W. Dykema, and how America's entry into the World War led to the larger pamphlet, the *Liberty* edition. He also gave a history of the Service version of *The Star Spangled Banner*.

Eleanor Smith, chairman of the committee on Sunday School Hymnal reported the completion of their work in the publication of *The Children's Hymnal*.

To assist the president of the Conference in keeping in touch with every section of the country a new committee began to function in the preparation for this meeting, entitled the President's Advisory Committee, consisting of all the state chairmen.

The following paragraphs regarding *The Star Spangled Banner* are from Mr. Dykema's report referred to above:—

"In the *Liberty* Edition there appeared a new arrangement of *The Star Spangled Banner* called the Service version. Although there has been presented in our official *Journal* some explanations of the reasons for this version, interest in the subject is so keen that a restatement with some additions may well be made at this time."

"About no other of our national songs has there been so much discussion as about *The Star Spangled Banner*. The fact that the War Department has designated it as our national anthem gives it a place of greatest importance. But there are other reasons which have caused the discussion. What is the proper version? If there were an official version brought forth and sanctioned by Congress or some equally authorized power, probably this uncertainty would disappear. Up to the present, however, no such action has been taken. We have therefore many versions of our national anthem. The printing of another requires an explanation."

"When in 1913, at the Rochester meeting, the Music Supervisors National Conference inaugurated the movement already mentioned for getting a few songs sung by all the people of the country, *The Star Spangled Banner* was naturally included in the list. At that time the spirit of loyalty led the editors of *Eighteen Songs for Community Singing* which was the pamphlet issued to forward this object, to adopt the version of this song which had been formulated some time before by a committee of the National

Education Association. After over a year of experiments with this version, the editors were forced to conclude that it was not a satisfactory one and they consequently made some modifications of the chorus. These modifications were so favorably received and criticisms of the unmodified verse portion continued so violent that the editors decided to consider for the new version of *Fifty-five Community Songs* (which had succeeded our original eighteen) a thoroughly revised version."

"While they were engaged in their discussions, they learned that a committee was working on a version of the song for inclusion in the *Army Song Book* to be issued by the War Department Commission on Training Camp Activities. Moreover, they were informed that several of the music publishing houses were still undecided as to the version they should use in their publication. The Committee of the Music Supervisors National Conference, realizing the desirability of uniformity in the version to be published by these different agencies, invited representatives of these interests to unite with them in their discussions. A joint committee was formed consisting of John A. Carpenter, Frederick S. Converse, Wallace Goodrich, Walter R. Spaulding, representing the War Department Commission of Training Camp Activities; Hollis E. Dann, Peter W. Dykema, Osbourne McConathy, representing the Music Supervisors National Conference; Clarence C.

Birchard, Carl Engel, Wm. Arms Fisher, Arthur E. Johnstone, and E. W. Newton, representing music publishers."

"Two courses are open to anyone who desires to make a version of *The Star Spangled Banner*, depending on the way he regards this song. If he considers it as a piece of music which obtained unchangeable form when it was originally written, his task is simply to consult the original sources and to decide which one of these most nearly expresses the composer's idea. For this purpose, Mr. Oscar Sonneck has placed at our disposal a scholarly history of *The Star Spangled Banner* which has been published by the Library of Congress. If, on the other hand, he decides that the song belongs to the people and like all folk songs, is subject to modification, his problem is to study the way in which the masses sing the song. This means that the material is not considered as fixed but fluid; that the song may have changed from its original form and may be subject to further modifications as the years go on. (An examination of the oldest published material shows that every version used today has changed greatly from the original form.) This latter point of view, that the song is a living, developing creation of the people, is the one which animated the joint Committee of Twelve."

"In order to determine what the people of America were singing, careful observation was made upon a great number of singers in many parts of the country. While both men and women in separate and in mixed groups were observed, special studies were made of those splendid examples of our fine representative manhood, the soldiers of the great camps. The Army and Navy Song Leaders were asked to gather their men in groups of various sizes and to start them singing *The Star Spangled Banner* and to allow them to finish it without conducting and without accompaniment. The Song Leaders were then to jot down the version as it emerged from the masses and to send in their data to the Committee. While, naturally there were many divergencies in this group singing, there were a few striking facts that emerged. One is that the American people emphasize their rhythm by using freely the unequally divided beat. Whether or not this is connected with their liking for ragtime may be a debatable question, but it seems, as one observer put it, that our people in the singing of *The Star Spangled Banner* at least, dot a note almost every time they have a chance. The N. E. A. version, therefore, which had been used in the original *Eighteen Songs* was an academic rather than a real simplifying of the song by wiping out the dotted eighth and quarter notes, because instead of making it more simple for our people to sing, it made it more difficult because more foreign to our natural tendencies."

"The story of the deliberations of this Commit-

tee of Twelve is one of many hours of investigation
and discussion.   From the conferences and a vast
amount of correspondence, came the version as
printed.   The determining of the melody by following the folk song idea was a comparatively easy
problem.   The committee was unanimous regarding
the version of the melody.   The question of the
harmony could not so easily be determined by reference to the singing of the people, because with us at
least, *The Star Spangled Banner* is essentially a
unison song.   The committee had difficulty in arriv-
ing at a suitable harmonization.   Especially marked
were differences of opinion regarding the treatment
of the first four measures of the chorus.   Protracted
discussion failed to bring about a unanimous opinion
as to the best bass for this portion (naturally with
corresponding tenor and alto).   However, the version finally selected received the support of a decided
majority of the members."[1]

In 1920 the Conference met at Philadelphia, and
the membership jumped suddenly from 646 in 1919
to 1242, a gain of 92 percent.   One of the most
important questions considered was that of the future
policy of the Conference.   After a report on the
question by a committee of past-presidents it was
voted to continue the policy of "national work for
higher standards, better co-ordination, and stronger

[1]*Book of Proceedings, Music Supervisors National Conference—*
1919, page 145.

organization for effective service to the 25,000,000 children in our public schools, and to favor and support state organizations and sectional conferences."

The Philadelphia meeting revealed the fact that the size of the Conference was becoming a problem in itself, and that it was no longer a simple matter to seat the entire body in one room. The program provided for ten section-meetings.

At the meeting at St. Joseph, Missouri, in 1921, an orchestra composed of conference members had a share for the first time in the annual concert under the direction of Will Earhart. The growing importance of instrumental music was evident in the program of the meeting, not only in papers and discussions, but in the large number of visiting school orchestras and bands.

The Educational Council made an extended report which later was printed and published as *Bulletin Number One*, and contained a basic four-year course for the training of music supervisors, and a *Standard Course in Music for the Elementary Grades*. This course was formulated by harmonizing the differences of opinion and uniting points of agreement among the members of the Council. Thus was settled, by the authority of a National body, through its own representatives, a question which had agitated the field of school-music for fifty years.

At this meeting George Oscar Bowen was elected

vice-president, which office included the editorship of the *Music Supervisors' Journal.*

The Committee on Necrology reported the death of E. L. Coburn, Nellie Elrod, Edward Futterer, Frances B. Gardiner, Jessie L. Gaynor, Esta Hungerford and N. Coe Stewart. The Conference sang *The Slumber Boat* by Jessie L. Gaynor as a tribute to her memory.

Clarence C. Birchard gave a eulogy of E. L. Coburn of which the following is the closing paragraph;—"Mr. Coburn showed many qualities which are the mark, even if not generally recognized, of these times, and especially characteristic in our American civilization,—rugged strength and straight forwardness, a rare kindliness, generosity and open-mindedness, a surprising freedom from rancor, a forgiving spirit, and ability to be misunderstood and to acknowledge wrong, a belief in the essential quality and goodness of human nature, a desire to unite people in the happy bond of peace and brotherhood, a capacity to win people from motives and through acts of aggressive friendliness, long-suffering confidence and belief in his friends, a constitutional and never-failing optimism, a ready wit, a crowd psychology, a social vision which gave him a far-off goal to work to, and an impersonal attitude of mind in matters involving service for the common good."

C. H. Congdon paid the following tribute to

N. Coe Stewart;—"I am sure that a great many of us remember Mr. Stewart. He was director of music in the public schools of Cleveland, Ohio, for a great many years. He was one of the leaders in public school music and represented that class of music leader in the school which included in its list the names of such men as George F. Root, H. R. Palmer and Lowell Mason. Mr. Stewart was one of the forward-looking men, and in his day the great exhibitions that he gave in Cleveland have almost gone down in the history of that city. Mr. Stewart's was a fine example of singing in the schools, singing by the people and singing of all kinds."

At the meeting in 1922, at Nashville, Tennessee, the membership numbered 1800. The Educational Council submitted a report on *High School Credits for Applied Music Study*, which was published as *Bulletin No. 2*.

The High School Orchestra from Richmond, Indiana, numbering about 75 players, under the direction of Joseph E. Maddy performed with remarkable finish and intonation the following program;—*Overture to Rienzi*—Wagner; *Andante Cantabile from Fifth Symphony*—Tschaikowsky; *Valse Triste*—Sibelius; *Praeludium*—Jarnefelt; *Hymn and Triumphal March* from Aida—Verdi.

From this meeting also dates the first committee on instrumental affairs, consisting of Jay W. Fay, chairman, Victor L. F. Rebmann, B. F. Stuber,

Russell V. Morgan and Eugene Hahnel.   Also a committee on Vocal Music consisting of Edgar B. Gordon, chairman, Mabelle Glenn, D. R. Gebhart, Ernest G. Hesser, Mary Nugent and J. Powell Jones.

As part of the report of the Committee on Necrology, C. H. Congdon, chairman, newspaper accounts were read concerning the death of William Alfred White, Director of Music in the schools of Denver, Colorado; Burton True Scales, Director of the Department of Music of Girard College, Philadelphia; Miss Caroline A. Strong, Warren, Ohio, and Miss Marie Leary, Supervisor of Music in Memphis, Tennessee.

In 1923, at the meeting at Cleveland the membership exceeded 2200.   At this meeting occurred the first Pioneers' Breakfast, bringing together as far as possible the original Keokuk group, with Frances E. Clark, the first Chairman of the Conference, as hostess.

The constitution was amended so as to increase the National Research Council of Music Education (the new name for the Educational Council) to fifteen members.   The Conference elected the following to the Council;—Will Earhart, Karl W. Gehrkens, Peter W. Dykema, Osbourne McConathy, Glenn Woods, Charles H. Farnsworth, Paul J. Weaver, Thaddeus P. Giddings, Hollis E. Dann, W. Otto Miessner, George H. Gartlan, Charles H. Miller,

Frank A. Beach, Frances E. Clark and John W. Beattie.

In 1924, at the meeting at Cincinnati the program included thirteen sectional meetings devoted to music in the grades, the rural schools, the junior and senior high schools, piano classes, voice instruction, the orchestra, the band, music appreciation, harmony, training of the grade teacher, the instrumental teacher, and the music supervisor.

Reports were approved from the Committee on Instrumental Music, Jay W. Fay, Chairman; National Music Week Committee, Clara E. Sanford, Chairman; and from five new committees, namely, Committee on Division of Responsibilities, John W. Beattie, Chairman; Book Shelf Committee, Paul J. Weaver, Chairman; Committee on Sectional Conferences, Peter W. Dykema, Chairman; Committee on National Conservatory, Osbourne McConathy, Chairman; and Committee on Tests and Measurements, Peter W. Dykema, Chairman.

Resolutions were passed concerning the deaths of Henry M. Butler, Julia Ettie Crane, J. Powell Jones and Marie Burt Parr.

In 1925, the Conference met at Kansas City, Missouri, with about 3000 members. At this meeting there was an unusually comprehensive exhibition of all types of music work carried on in the Kansas City schools, consisting of grade work in singing and reading, music appreciation, harmony, piano classes, all kinds of instrumental work, together with very effective massed singing by primary, elementary and high school grades in the large Convention Hall, under the direction of Mabelle Glenn.

The Research Council presented a report on *Junior High School Music* which was published as *Bulletin No. 4*, and *A Standard Course of Training in Music for Grade Teachers*, which was published as *Bulletin No. 5*.

The Conference voted to change from annual to biennial meetings, beginning the new plan in 1926, meeting thus on even years. The Eastern and Southern Conferences had voted previously to change to the biennial plan, beginning in 1927 and meeting the odd years.

A brief memorial service was held for members who had passed on during the year;—Henry W. Fairbanks, Anna Costello, Mrs. Charles H. Miller, Philip C. Hayden, Elwood L. Philbrick and Jessie L. Clark.

The meeting at Detroit in 1926 was the first held on the biennial plan. A new constitution was adopted providing for the biennial meetings and for the co-ordination of the National Conference with the Sectional Conferences, the main feature of this relation being that members of the Sectional Conferences become automatically members also of the National Conference. It was provided that there should be one *Book of Proceedings* for all, and one

Journal, and that one half of the membership dues should be set aside for the *Book of Proceedings.*

Two new sectional Conferences were organized, namely the North Central and the Southwestern.

At a brief memorial service tributes to the memory of Philip C. Hayden were given by William Kinnear and Karl W. Gehrkens. Mr. Walter Butterfield spoke briefly of the life work of Charles S. Conant of Concord, New Hampshire, and Osbourne McConathy of the outstanding life work of Samuel W. Cole of Brookline, Massachusetts. The tributes to Philip C. Hayden were as follows;—

PHILIP CADY HAYDEN
by K. W. Gehrkens, Oberlin, Ohio

"Philip Cady Hayden was born in Brantford, Ontario, Canada, in 1854. He studied in New York University one year and in Oberlin College five years. After leaving Oberlin he became supervisor of music in Quincy, Illinois, and later in Keokuk, Iowa. His work as a music teacher in the public schools covered a period of thirty-five years. In 1900, he founded the magazine *School Music,* at first called *School Music Monthly.* A few years later he issued the call that led to the organization of the Music Supervisors National Conference. He died May 15, 1925.

"Mr. Hayden was a pioneer, an experimenter. He was willing to try a thing even though it had never been done before. He was known and loved by a host of men and women throughout the United States. His contribution to the cause of Public School Music will bulk larger and larger as the years go by."

PHILIP CADY HAYDEN

by William B. Kinnear, McPherson College,

McPherson, Kansas.

"Interest in P. C. Hayden, for school music supervisors, revolves around the most conspicuous service of his last two decades and more of life.

"Earnestly active as secretary of the N. E. A. Music Department, he knew intimately the men and women who were struggling to bring the cause of school-music to the attention of educational leaders and the country at large.   He sensed the need of an organ of communication between members of his educational group.   With a sublime faith in the worthiness of his cause, and with the spirit and daring of the true pioneer, he launched out into the unknown in the first issue of a little magazine bearing the name of *School Music Monthly*.   This was in 1900.

"Those fortunate enough to possess complete files of this magazine may recall with what anxious hope the venture was made.   Subscriptions came very gradually, but in sufficient volume eventually to permit continuance.   At the time of its beginning, this was the only publication devoted exclusively to public school music.   Factors contributing to success were publication in a small city, making possible a subscription price in keeping with modest incomes of supervisors of those days, and an editorial catholicity permitting free exploiting of all shades of opinion.

"A second claim to distinction as a public benefactor in the cause of education was Mr. Hayden's activity in the call for the Keokuk meeting, out of which grew the Music Supervisors' National Conference. To endure the narrow and almost vicious criticism at that first meeting, and yet keep sweet and loyal to the cause in the direction taken by events, revealed a character that challenges admiration, and deserves to be held in appreciative remembrance by his companions in service."

The most remarkable feature of the 1926 meeting was the performance of the National High School Orchestra under the direction of Joseph E. Maddy and Ossip Gabrilovitch. The playing of this orchestra was a revelation of adolescent team work, applied to musical proportion, balance, tone color, intonation and rhythm. Equally it was a revelation of the extent of instrumental instruction throughout the country. The orchestra was assembled from over thirty states including Maine and California, and the membership represented 121 different orchestras.

The meeting at Chicago April 15-20, 1928 was the first under the biennial plan. The registration showed an actual attendance of over forty-six hundred, while the membership as reported by President Bowen was upwards of fifty-four hundred.   With the exception of four concerts, all the meetings were held at the Stevens Hotel, whose facilities were ample enough to house with comfort the largest gathering of music educators ever held.

The year 1928 marked the coming of age of the National Conference, dating from the initial meeting at Keokuk in 1907.   This fact was recognized by a complimentary breakfast to the original Keokuk group by the entire Conference body at which Percy Scholes, of London, presented a book of greetings from the musicians of Great Britain.   Through the efforts of Mr. Scholes, plans were formulated for an international gathering in Europe for the furthering of international understanding and fellowship.   (The first meeting of the international group was held in London June 7, 1928, at which it was decided to hold an International Conference in Switzerland in 1929.)

The week's program at Chicago was rich and varied, including general and sectional meetings, banquets and many concerts.   The musical performances reached an artistic level above that attained at any previous meeting.   Besides the complimentary concerts by the Chicago Symphony Orchestra, the Chicago Little Symphony Orchestra, the Chicago Bach Chorus and the A Cappella Choir of Northwestern University, fine programs were given by the A Cappella High School Chorus of Flint, Michigan, the

Presidents of the Music Supervisors' National Conference

FRANCES E. CLARK

PHILIP C. HAYDEN

E. L. COBURN

EDWARD B. BIRGE

CHARLES A. FULLERTON

ARTHUR W. MASON

Presidents of the
Music Supervisors' National Conference

WILL EARHART

PETER W. DYKEMA

OSBOURNE McCONATHY

CHARLES H. MILLER

JOHN W. BEATTIE

HOLLIS E. DANN

FRANK A. BEACH

KARL W. GEHRKENS

W. OTTO MIESSNER

WILLIAM BREACH

EDGAR B. GORDON

GEORGE OSCAR BOWEN

Presidents of the
North Central Music Supervisors' Conference

ANTON H. EMBS

ADA BICKING

HERMAN F. SMITH

WILLIAM W. NORTON

FOWLER SMITH

CAROL M. PITTS

Lodi-Leroy Little Symphony Orchestra, recruited from rural schools in and about the towns of Lodi and Leroy in Ohio, the Chicago High Schools Orchestra, the Chicago High Schools A Cappella Chorus and other Chicago groups. The National High School Orchestra of two hundred and eighty-three players made its third appearance as an organization, playing superbly under the direction of Frederick Stock, Howard Harold Hanson and Joseph E. Maddy, the organizer of the orchestra. The new feature of the Conference was the National High School Chorus of three hundred, which sang faultlessly under the direction of Hollis Dann a program of *a cappella* and concerted music accompanied by sixty members of the Chicago Symphony Orchestra.

(A significant outgrowth of the work of the National High School Orchestra was the planning and successful inauguration, under the leadership of Mr. Maddy, of a summer National High School Orchestra Camp, located near Traverse City, Michigan, which provides for eight weeks of intensive instruction from a faculty of twenty artist teachers and weekly concert performances under the foremost orchestral conductors.)

The National Research Council presented two completed reports, one a *Study of College Entrance Requirements and College Courses in Music*, to be published as *Bulletin No. 8*, and the other a report on *Standards of Attainment for Sight-Singing at the*

End of the Sixth Grade, to be published as *Bulletin No. 9*.

At the business meeting the following were elected to the Research Council for the five-year period 1928 to 1933: T. P. Giddings, W. Otto Miessner, Victor L. F. Rebmann; the following were elected for the five-year period 1929-1934: George Oscar Bowen, Ada Bicking, Hollis Dann. The personnel of the Council at the Chicago meeting was as follows: Peter Dykema, Chairman, Frank A. Beach, John W. Beattie, Edward B. Birge, Walter Aiken, Edgar B. Gordon, George H. Gartlan, Russell V. Morgan, Mabelle Glenn, C. A. Fullerton, Karl W. Gehrkens, Osbourne McConathy, Glenn Woods, Charles H. Farnsworth.

The committee on Necrology called attention to the deaths of Charles H. Congdon, of New York City, Charles I. Rice, of Worcester, Massachusetts, and Agnes C. Heath of Chicago. Brief tributes to their life work were given by Edward B. Birge, Ralph L. Baldwin and Frances E. Clark.

THE LAUSANNE CONFERENCE

The First Anglo-American Music Conference was held at Lausanne, Switzerland, August 2-9, 1929. It was attended by about 150 Americans and twice as many more from England, Scotland, Wales, Irish Free State, Ulster, Canada, Australia, New Zealand, South Africa, Ceylon and Germany. The gathering

was made possible through the tireless efforts of
Percy Scholes and his efficient co-workers in England
and America. Sir Henry Hadow was the chief pre-
siding officer. The programs included representative
speakers from England and America followed by discussions. So successful was the undertaking that a
committee was appointed to arrange for a second
International Music Conference in 1931.

Second Biennial Meeting

The National Conference held its second biennial in Chicago March 23-28, 1930, with a total membership of 7505. At this meeting a new constitution
was adopted, providing for placing the business
affairs of the Conference in the hands of an "executive secretary," a new official, and discontinuing the
old offices of Secretary, Treasurer and Auditor.
Clifford V. Buttelman was appointed executive secretary. The new constitution enlarges the scope of
the Conference by making eligible for membership
anyone interested in music education whether officially connected with public schools or not.

Both in attendance and in the strength of the
program the third biennial meeting was outstanding.
This was especially true of the musical programs,
which in recent years have become the central feature
of the Conference meetings. High-level performances of great music were given by the National High
School Chorus under Hollis Dann and the National

High School Orchestra under Joseph E. Maddy, The Flint A Cappella Choir under Jacob A. Evanson, the Glenville High School Choral Club under Griffith J. Jones, and the Omaha Central High School Glee Clubs under Carol Machoff Pitts.

Third Biennial Meeting

The National Conference held its third biennial April 3-8, 1932, in Cleveland. This was the silver anniversary meeting, dating from the birth of the Conference at Keokuk, Iowa, in 1907. A festival atmosphere prevailed throughout the week. As at previous meetings, choruses, bands and orchestras, large and small, gave of their best. The Music Discrimination Contest, sponsored by the Music Appreciation Committee and the National Broadcasting Company was an innovation. It was a fine demonstration of some results to be expected of courses in music appreciation, when conducted by thoroughly qualified teachers. Another innovation was a Pageant of American Music in the Community, showing our early American music, native resources, gifts from other nations, and the present opportunities.

Fourth Biennial Meeting

At the fourth biennial, held in Chicago April 8-13, 1934, it was voted to change the name of the Music Supervisors' National Conference to Music Educators National Conference and the name Music

Supervisors' Journal to Music Educators Journal. In spite of the "depression" the attendance was very large. Instead of a National High School Chorus, a National Supervisors Chorus sang under the direction of Hollis Dann. A special new feature of the meeting was the importance given to demonstrations of small instrumental ensembles, and to a high school solo singing contest sponsored by the Committee on Vocal Affairs and the American Academy of Teachers of Singing.

Fifth Biennial Meeting

The fifth biennial, held in New York City March 29-April 3, 1936, under the presidency of Herman F. Smith, was noteworthy for the smooth functioning of conference committees. The meetings were carefully planned and efficiently carried out. The program listed 114 separate events, with the principal sessions taking place in the Metropolitan Opera House. Other meetings and concerts were held in the ballrooms of the Hotel Pennsylvania, The New Yorker, McAlpin and Governor Clinton, and in Carnegie Hall, Center Theater, N B C Broadcasting Studios, Juilliard School of Music Auditorium, and Madison Square Garden. Speakers, conductors, session chairmen and others listed as participants totaled 302. The registered members numbered 6625, but the total attendance at all the meetings was 39,300

The performances by visiting organizations such as the Joliet Township High School Band, the combined High School Choirs of Rochester, and the John Adams (Cleveland) High School Orchestra were all on the highest level of excellence.   A special performance at the Metropolitan Opera House of *Lohengrin* was arranged by the management of the Opera House. The "New York Night" Concert and that of the Associated Glee Clubs of America at Madison Square Garden were magnificent spectacles and delightful to both sight and hearing.   The Folk Festival at the Metropolitan Opera House on Friday night furnished a fitting climax for the week.

Other important features of this memorable conference meeting were the Exhibitors' exposition, the visits to the broadcasting studios, the voice, piano, band and orchestra clinics held daily, and the presentation of "Scientific Aids to Music Education" at Center Theater, Radio City, including the first public performance of the music composed by Kurt Weill for Max Reinhardt's *Eternal Road*, demonstrating at a "preview" the new ultra-violet sound film.

At the biennial business meeting Joseph E. Maddy was elected president for 1937-1938.

The Music Supervisors' Journal

One of the most important factors in the growth and efficiency of the National Conference has been the *Music Supervisors' Journal*, its official organ.

Established in 1914 and issued quarterly under the title *Music Supervisors' Bulletin*, (changed in 1916 to the *Music Supervisors' Journal*), and with the broad and far-sighted policy of reaching the entire constituency of school-music, it has kept the plans and problems of the Conference constantly before all the supervisors of the country. Thus through the *Journal* The National Conference has, in a sense, been in continuous session. In its pages the work of standing committees has been given full expression, especially that of the Instrumental and the Tests and Measurements Committees, as have various urgent problems of policy and organization. It is doubtful if the change from annual to biennial meetings with the necessary adjustments with the Sectional Conferences could have been so swiftly and successfully consummated without the help of the *Journal*. The magazine has had three editors; Peter W. Dykema from 1914 to 1921, George Oscar Bowen from 1921 to 1926, and Paul J. Weaver who became editor at the Detroit meeting in 1926. From 1917, the office of Second Vice-President carried with it the editorship of the *Journal*. With the adoption of the new constitution at the 1930 meeting, the editor of the *Journal* is appointed by the executive committee.

CALENDAR OF MEETINGS

1907 Keokuk, Iowa (Organized)
Frances E. Clark,
Chairman
P. C. Hayden, *Secretary*

1909 Indianapolis, Indiana
P. C. Hayden, *President*
Stella R. Root, *Secretary*

1910 Cincinnati, Ohio
E. L. Coburn, *President*
Stella R. Root, *Secretary*

1911 Detroit, Michigan
Edward B. Birge,
President
Clyde E. Foster, *Secretary*

1912 St. Louis, Missouri
Charles A. Fullerton,
President
M. Ethel Hudson,
Secretary

1913 Rochester, New York
Henrietta G. Baker,
President
Helen Cook, *Secretary*

1914 Minneapolis, Minnesota
Elizabeth Casterton,
President
May E. Kimberly,
Secretary

1915 Pittsburg, Pennsylvania
Arthur W. Mason,
President
Charles H. Miller,
Secretary

1916 Lincoln, Nebraska
Will Earhart, *President*
Agnes Benson, *Secretary*

1917 Grand Rapids, Michigan
Peter W. Dykema,
President
Julia E. Crane, *Secretary*

1918 Evansville, Indiana
Charles H. Miller,
President
Ella M. Brownell,
Secretary

1919 St. Louis, Missouri
Osbourne McConathy,
President
Mabelle Glenn, *Secretary*

1920 Philadelphia, Pennsylvania
Hollis E. Dann, *President*
Elizabeth Pratt, *Secretary*

1921 St. Joseph, Missouri
John W. Beattie, *President*
E. Jane Wisenall,
Secretary

1922 Nashville, Tennessee
Frank A. Beach, *President*
Ada Bicking, *Secretary*

1923 Cleveland, Ohio
Karl W. Gehrkens,
President
Alice Jones, *Secretary*

1924 Cincinnati, Ohio
W. Otto Miessner,
President
Winifred V. Smith,
Secretary

1925 Kansas City, Missouri
William Breach, *President*
Grace V. Wilson,
Secretary

1926 Detroit, Michigan
Edgar B. Gordon, *President*
Mrs. Elizabeth Carmichael, *Secretary*

1928 Chicago, Illinois
George Oscar Bowen,
President
Mrs. Marian E. Cotton,
Secretary

1930 Chicago, Illinois
Mabelle Glenn, *President*
Sadie Rafferty, *Secretary*

1932 Cleveland, Ohio
Russell V. Morgan,
President
Clifford V. Buttelman,
Executive Secretary

1934 Chicago, Illinois
Walter H. Butterfield,
President
Clifford V. Buttelman,
Executive Secretary

1936 New York City
Herman F. Smith,
President
Clifford V. Buttelman,
Executive Secretary

The Eastern Music Supervisors' Conference

By Edwin N. C. Barnes

(Used by permission of Dr. Barnes, editor and publisher of
Who's Who in Music Education)

"The Eastern Music Supervisors' Conference is the outgrowth of certain activities on the part of a number of members of the Pulse Club of Boston and a group of Eastern Music Educators who attended the session of the Music Supervisors' National Conference at Grand Rapids, Michigan, in the spring of 1917. Prominent in the Pulse Club group were Howard C. Davis of Chelsea, Massachusetts, and Richard W. Grant of Winchester, Massachusetts. During the journey home from Grand Rapids, Frederick W. Archibald of Waltham, Massachusetts, called together the second named group and presented the urgent need of an Eastern organization.

"Later in the spring the Pulse Club issued a call in which Mr. Archibald concurred, for a meeting of all interested at Nantasket, Massachusetts. At this meeting at which Mr. Davis presided, the whole matter of organization was thoroughly discussed— encouraging addresses were given by Payson Smith, Commissioner of Education for Massachusetts and Emerson L. Adams, Deputy Commissioner of Education for Rhode Island. Among others the writer was called upon to outline his thought of the aim and work of such a conference. A permanent committee, charged with the duty of organization, was elected at this meeting. This committee included Samuel W. Cole, of Brookline, Massachusetts; Mr. Davis, Mr. Grant, Walter H. Butterfield of Manchester, New Hampshire; Albert Edmund Brown of the Lowell (Massachusetts) Normal School; Mary McCormack of Providence, Rhode Island; Esther Green of the Keene, New Hampshire, Normal School; James D. Price of Hartford, Connecticut; the writer and others.

"At a meeting at Boston in the fall, organization was effected under the name of the Eastern Music Supervisors' Conference and the following officers were elected: Albert Edmund Brown of Lowell, Massachusetts, President; Ralph L. Baldwin of Hartford, Connecticut, First Vice-President; Edwin N. C. Barnes of Central Falls, Rhode Island, Second Vice-President and editor of the conference paper; Richard W. Grant of Winchester, Massachusetts, Secretary; James D. Price of Hartford, Connecticut,

Treasurer; Samuel W. Cole of Brookline, Massachusetts, Counselor, and Walter H. Butterfield of Manchester, New Hampshire, Auditor.

"George T. Goldthwaite, Portland, Maine, was made chairman of the board of directors, the other members being;—Esther M. Greene, Keene, New Hampshire; Charles E. Wood, Springfield, Vermont; Charles I. Rice, Worcester, Massachusetts; and Mary T. McCormack, Providence, Rhode Island.

"Much hard work was done by the officers during the winter and when the first session met in Boston, May, 1918 there were over 400 in attendance from New England, New York, New Jersey and even Virginia. It was a good session, virile and stirring, with a fine constructive program. The infant seemed a lusty one indeed and all were very sanguine as to its enjoying a splendid and useful life.

"The original thought was to make the conference local, covering simply New England, New York and New Jersey. The name Eastern implied more than that, however, and prior to the initial meeting at Boston, through the efforts of the writer, the territory was extended to include all the Atlantic seaboard states and West Virginia on the south and the Canadian Maritime provinces, New Brunswick, Nova Scotia and Prince Edward Island on the north. Conference representatives were secured in each state and province. In the fall of 1918 the name of the conference paper, was at the suggestion of the editor, changed from the *Eastern Music Supervisors' Bulletin* to the *Eastern School Music Herald*."

THE EASTERN MUSIC SUPERVISORS' CONFERENCE

By Richard W. Grant

"One cannot write of the beginnings of the Eastern Music Supervisors' Conference without mentioning in the same breath the "Pulse Club," which was organized in Boston and incorporated under the laws of Massachusetts on February 13, 1915. Membership in the Club has been open to Supervisors of Public School Music in the New England States. Since all the meetings have been held in Boston, however, most of the active work was of necessity done by the members living in and about greater Boston.

"The charter members of the Club included James M. McLaughlin, then director of music in Boston, B. Harold Hamblin, assistant director of music in Boston, Percy Graham, then director in Lynn, John B. Whoriskey, director of music in Cambridge, W. G. Boston, then director in Webster, Mass., Howard Clarke Davis, of Chelsea, and Richard W. Grant, then director of music in Winchester. It was their intention that the corporation be constituted for the purpose of educational advancement in school music, and of promoting good fellowship and encouragement among its members. That these intentions have been realized can best be attested by stating that the Eastern Music Supervisors' Conference is a child of the Pulse Club, for it was conceived in the minds of certain members of the Club, as I will attempt to explain. Incidentally the "child" has grown to be quite a husky kid and is much larger than its mother.

"It might be interesting to relate briefly the incidents leading up to the formation of the conference. At a meeting of the Pulse Club held in Boston, on March 10, 1917, it was the unanimous desire of those present to extend an invitation to the National Music Supervisors' Conference to hold its 1918 meeting in Boston. It was realized that there were many problems in school music which could best be discussed by the gathering together of a larger group of people of the same profession with varied experience in the realm of music. Howard Clarke Davis, then president of the Club, had devoted a large part of his time during the winter to procuring written invitations from Superintendents of Schools and Music Supervisors of greater Boston. The data were obtained and bound in an attractive booklet and included not only invitations from his Excellency, the Governor of Massachusetts, the Mayor of Boston, the President of the Chamber of Commerce, the Commissioner of Education, but also invitations from thirty school systems within a radius of ten miles of Boston, the aggregate population of which was 1,558,933 with a school attendance of 261,866 children. It was decided that a committee should personally carry this composite invitation to the National Conference, which convened in 1917 at Grand Rapids, Mich. Accordingly Percy Graham, of Lynn, and the writer, armed with this formidable document, set forth for Grand Rapids and by dint of much labor sold the idea of a Boston conference for 1918 by obtaining a majority vote at the annual business meeting. Afterwards the Executive Committee of the conference barred the invitation on the ground that the educational authorities of the City of Boston had not directly included theirs. This was a fact and the action of the Committee was perfectly proper.

"A number of New England people were at this meeting, and on the return journey an impromptu gathering on the train voiced the general sentiment of the need of a conference that would be geographically accessible to supervisors in the East. A leader in this consultation was F. W. Archibald, director of music in the Normal Schools of Framingham and Salem, but his idea as well as the others included only a New England Conference.

"If credit for the idea of an Eastern Supervisors' Conference is to be given, let it go to Howard C. Davis, who broached the subect to me one evening during an informal visit at his home. This was in the late winter of 1917. It was subsequently discussed at meetings of the Pulse Club, and finally an invitation was sent to representative supervisors in the New

Presidents of the
Southwestern Music Supervisors' Conference

MABELLE GLENN

JOHN C. KENDAL

GRACE V. WILSON

FRANCES SMITH CATRON

Presidents of the
Eastern Music Supervisors' Conference

ALBERT EDMUND BROWN

RALPH L. BALDWIN

HOWARD C. DAVIS

GEORGE H. GARTLAN

HARRY E. WHITTEMORE

JAMES D. PRICE

LOUISE WESTWOOD

RICHARD W. GRANT

GEORGE J. ABBOTT

VICTOR L. F. REBMANN

ELBRIDGE S. PITCHER

Presidents of the
Eastern Music Supervisors' Conference

M. CLAUDE ROSENBERRY

RALPH G. WINSLOW

LAURA BRYANT

GEORGE L. LINDSAY

England States to attend a meeting on June 9, 1917, at Nantasket Beach, for the purpose of considering the advisability of organizing such a conference. Fifty people responded, representing every New England State. The group at Nantasket voted unanimously to organize, and a committe of two from each of the six New England States were elected with H. C. Davis as temporary chairman and R. W. Grant as temporary secretary. At this meeting it was made plain that the Eastern Conference was not in any way antagonistic to the National Conference, and that it was the intention to co-operate with the larger body to the fullest extent.

"This sub-committee then met in Boston on October 13, 1917, and formed a permanent organization to be known as the Eastern Music Supervisors' Conference. Mr. Davis had in the meantime been appointed Director of Music in Yonkers, N. Y., and felt it was necessary for him to resign as temporary chairman, because of living so far away. At this committee meeting a new temporary chairman was elected, who in turn appointed a nominating committee of three, consisting of Miss Mary T. McCormack of Providence, R. I., Charles E. Wood of Springfield, Vermont, and James D. Price of Hartford, Conn. This committee nominated the following officers who were unanimously elected: Albert Edmund Brown of Lowell, Mass., President; Ralph L. Baldwin of Hartford, Conn., First Vice-President; Edwin N. C.

Barnes, Central Falls, R. I., Second Vice-President and Editor, Richard W. Grant, Winchester, Mass., Secretary; James D. Price, Hartford, Conn., Treasurer, and George W. Goldthwaite, Portland, Maine, Chairman of the Board of Directors. A temporary constitution and by-laws were adopted; the method of financing was agreed on, which incidentally included a voluntary assessment on each officer in order to assure a successful start; Boston was chosen as the meeting place; the dates were set for May 8, 9, 10, and 11, 1918; and the first Eastern Conference was on its way.

"Then followed a period of intensive work on the part of the officers in order that this first conference should succeed. Too much credit cannot be given for the painstaking care that went into this. It was however, worth all the effort, for now that it is history, it is realized that this first meeting was not only outstanding as·regards attendance and the fine quality of the program, but it set the organization firmly on its feet financially and gave it a standing as one of the influential musical bodies of this country. In mentioning the early financing of the conference I think it is pertinent to recall a very important fact; namely, that a large part of this success was due to the willingness of the Music Publishing houses to advertise in our journal, *The Herald*. As I recall my visits to the various managers of these houses with a "dummy" *Herald* in my hand, with the conference months away, and with nothing but hopes for the future to offer, I cannot help reflecting that these men must have felt that they were taking a long chance with the firm's money. Many thanks to them; I hope they feel they have been well repaid.

Consequently the fine work of Edwin N. C. Barnes as editor is especially worthy of mention.

The Eastern Music Supervisors' Conference is now firmly established, and each passing year sees it wax bigger and stronger. To those of us who labored back in 1917 and 1918 it is a comforting thought to know that through this conference a generous contribution is being made to the uplift and advancement of the art we hold so dear. Let this good work go on and on."

(Editor) The first meeting under the biennial plan was at Worcester, Massachusetts, March 8-11, 1927.

EASTERN MUSIC SUPERVISORS' CONFERENCE
CALENDAR OF MEETINGS

1918 Boston, Massachusetts
Albert E. Brown,
 President
Richard W. Grant,
 Secretary

1919 Hartford, Connecticut
Ralph L. Baldwin,
 President
Esther M. Greene,
 Secretary

1920 New York City, New York
Howard C. Davis,
 President
Mary M. Shaw, *Secretary*

1921 Boston, Massachusetts
George H. Gartlan,
 President
Laura Bryant, *Secretary*

1922 Springfield, Massachusetts
Harry E. Whittemore,
 President
Pauline A. Meyer,
 Secretary

1923 Newark, New Jersey
James D. Price, *President*
Mary G. Nugent,
 Secretary

1924 Rochester, New York
Louise Westwood,
 President
Maude M. Howes,
 Secretary

1925 New Haven, Connecticut
Richard W. Grant,
 President
Betridge Tucker,
 Secretary

1926 Atlantic City, New Jersey
George J. Abbott, *President*
Bertha D. Hughes, *Secretary*

1927 Worcester, Massachusetts
Victor L. F. Rebmann, Yonkers, New York, *President*
Grace G. Pierce, Arlington, Massachusetts, *Secretary*

1929 Philadelphia, Pennsylvania
Elbridge S. Pitcher,
President
Grace G. Pierce, *Secretary*

1931 Syracuse, New York
M. Claude Rosenberry,
President
Marion Knightly Wilson,
Secretary

1933 Providence, Rhode Island
Ralph G. Winslow,
President
Elisabeth Gleason,
Secretary

1935 Pittsburgh, Pennsylvania
Laura Bryant, *President*
Anna L. McInerney,
Secretary

OFFICERS FOR 1935-1937

George L. Lindsay, *President*
Laura Bryant, *First Vice-President*
F. Colwell Conklin, *Second Vice-President*
Elizabeth V. Beach, *Secretary*
Clarence Wells, *Treasurer*
Laura Bryant, *Director*
Doris Rayner, *Director*
John W. Neff, *Director*
Lee M. Lockhart, *Director*

THE SOUTHERN CONFERENCE FOR MUSIC EDUCATION

By Paul J. Weaver

(Used by permission of Edwin N. C. Barnes, editor and publisher of *Who's Who in Music Education*)

"During the 1922 meeting of the Music Supervisors' National Conference at Nashville, Tennessee, a group of about 125 music teachers from the

Southeastern section of the United States organized themselves as a branch of the National Conference under the name of the Southern Music Supervisors' Conference. The purpose of the organization was to study music conditions and problems peculiar to the South and encourage a constructive program of music development in that great section of the country.

"Under the presidency of the writer, Director of Music at the University of North Carolina, Chapel Hill, North Carolina, the first annual meeting was held at Atlanta, Georgia, in November, 1922. The second meeting occurred in November, 1923 at Louisville, Kentucky, under the leadership of D. R. Gebhart of Peabody College, Nashville, Tennessee, as president. Miss Alice Bivins of the North Carolina College for Women was the third president and presided over the session at Winston-Salem, North Carolina, in November, 1924. The present president, (1925) is Miss Helen McBride, and the fourth session will be at Birmingham, Alabama.

"The Southern Conference has from its inception, included not only music supervisors, but also university, college and conservatory directors and teachers of music, and private music teachers. Believing the music upbuilding of the country could only be accomplished through the close association and cooperation of these different groups, the organization at the 1924 session, changed its name from the Southern Music Supervisors' Conference to the Southern Conference for Music Education. The body includes in its membership a large number of prominent music teachers from the thirteen Southeastern states and the District of Columbia. Its territory is bounded on the north by Virginia, the District of Columbia, West Virginia and Kentucky, and includes, to the west of the Mississippi river, Arkansas, Oklahoma and Texas.

"The 1924 session was marked by an outstanding achievement. Through the Committee on Educational Policy, the conference succeeded in obtaining the adoption of a standard course of music study for high schools. This course was later approved at the 1924 meeting of the Southern Association of Secondary Schools and Colleges. The new conference is most decidedly up and doing, and will, without doubt, do much for the musical emancipation of the Southland."

(Editor) The above sketch was written by Mr. Weaver in 1925. The following year the biennial conference plan was inaugurated, and two new sections, the North Central and Southwestern were organized. This necessitated some adjustment of territory among the various sections, with the following belonging to the Southern Conference: — District of Columbia, Virginia, West Virginia, Kentucky, Tennessee, North Carolina, South Carolina, Georgia, Florida, Alabama, Mississippi, and Maryland. The first meeting under the biennial plan was at Richmond, Virginia, April 4-8, 1927.

Presidents of the Southern Conference
for Music Education

PAUL J. WEAVER

DAVID R. GEBHART

ALICE E. BIVINS

HELEN McBRIDE

LEWIS L. STOOKEY

WILLIAM BREACH

GRACE P. WOODMAN

J. HENRY FRANCIS

GRACE VAN DYKE MORE

SOUTHERN CONFERENCE FOR MUSIC EDUCATION

CALENDAR OF MEETINGS

1922 Atlanta, Georgia
Paul J. Weaver, *President*
Alice Bivins, *Secretary*

1923 Louisville, Kentucky
David R. Gebhart,
President
Kate Lee Harralson,
Secretary

1924 Winston-Salem, N. C.
Alice Bivins, *President*
Elizabeth Bell, *Secretary*

1925 Birmingham, Alabama
(January 11-15, 1926)
Helen McBride, *President*
Jennie Belle Smith,
Secretary

1926 Richmond, Virginia (April 4-8, 1927)
L. L. Stookey, High Point, North Carolina, *President*
Irma Lee Batey, Alpine, Texas, *Secretary*

1929 Asheville, North Carolina
William Breach, *President*
Ella M. Hayes, *Secretary*

1931 Memphis, Tennessee
Grace P. Woodman,
President
Minnie D. Stensland,
Secretary

1933 Atlanta, Georgia (Meeting
postponed)
J. Henry Francis,
President
Jennie Belle Smith,
Secretary

1935 New Orleans, Louisiana
J. Henry Francis,
President
Jennie Belle Smith,
Secretary

OFFICERS FOR 1935-1937

Grace Van Dyke More, *President*

E. May Saunders, *First Vice-President*

Price Doyle, *Second Vice-President*

Georgia B. Wagner, *Secretary*

C. V. Buttelman, *Treasurer*

Mary B. Conway, *Director*

Lewis L. Stookey, *Director*

J. Henry Francis, *Director*

Southwestern Music Supervisors' Conference

Through the medium of a questionaire and vote, three members of an organization committee from eight states were appointed to meet in Detroit in 1926 at the Music Supervisors' National Conference, and organize the Southwestern Conference, to include Kansas, Missouri, Colorado, Arkansas, Oklahoma, Texas, New Mexico and Louisiana. Wyoming also applied for admission to this group and was accepted, the understanding being that she would later on belong to a Northwestern Conference.

The first biennial session of the new Conference was held at Tulsa, Oklahoma, the first week in March, 1927. The outstanding features were a concert in Convention Hall, given by the Southwest High School Chorus under the direction of George Oscar Bowen, the Southwest High School Orchestra under the direction of N. de Rubertis, conductor of the Kansas City Symphony Orchestra, and the dedication of the new organ in the High School. This organ was bought by the students as a memorial from the graduating classes of several successive years. The dedication program was played by Palmer Christian, assisted by Mr. Bowen's combined glee clubs. There was also a Music Appreciation Contest conducted by Margaret Lowry of Kansas City.

CALENDAR OF MEETINGS

1927 Tulsa, Oklahoma
    Mabelle Glenn, *President*
    Frank A. Beach, *Secretary*

1929 Wichita, Kansas
    John C. Kendel, *President*
    Mary M. Conway,
    Secretary

1931 Colorado Springs,
    Colorado
    Grace V. Wilson,
    President
    Sarah K. White, *Secretary*

1933 Springfield, Missouri
    (Meeting postponed)
    Frances Smith Catron,
    President
    Lena Milam, *Secretary*

1935 Springfield, Missouri
    Frances Smith Catron,
    President
    Lena Milam, *Secretary*

OFFICERS FOR 1935-1937

John C. Kendel, *President*
R. Ritchie Robertson, *First Vice-President*
James L. Waller, *Second Vice-President*
T. Frank Coulter, *Secretary*
Catharine E. Strouse, *Treasurer*
George Oscar Bowen, *Director*
Grace V. Wilson, *Director*

The North Central Music Supervisors' Conference

Some months before the first biennial meeting at Detroit in 1926 of the Music Supervisors' National Conference, the In-and-About-Chicago Supervisors' Club had named a committee with Anton H. Embs of Oak Park, Illinois as chairman to effect the organization of the North Central Conference to consist of the following states:—Ohio, Indiana, Illinois, Iowa, Nebraska, Wisconsin, Michigan, Minnesota, North Dakota and South Dakota.

The first biennial meeting of the new Conference was held at Springfield, Illinois, the week of April 11, 1927. In his president's address, Anton H. Embs asked some searching questions, speaking on the topic, "Public School Music; Education or Recreation?" At this conference was assembled the first Conference Symphonic Band, of High School students from the various states, directed by Lee Lockhart and A. R. McAllister. The band made a splendid impression, as did also the North Central Chorus, made up of two hundred and fifty three boys and girls from the high schools of eight states, and directed by Daniel Protheroe and Harry O. Ferguson.

CALENDAR OF MEETINGS

1927 Springfield, Illinois
   Anton H. Embs, *President*
   Alice Jones, *Secretary*

1929 Milwaukee, Wisconsin
   Ada Bicking, *President*
   Fannie C. Amidon,
      Secretary

1931 Des Moines, Iowa
   Herman F. Smith,
      President
   Edith M. Keller, *Secretary*

1933 Grand Rapids, Michigan
   William W. Norton,
      President
   Carol M. Pitts, *Secretary*

1935 Indianapolis, Indiana
   Fowler Smith, *President*
   Florence Flanagan,
      Secretary

OFFICERS FOR 1935-1937

Carol M. Pitts, *President*
Hobart H. Sommers, *First Vice-President*
Orien E. Dailey, *Second Vice-President*
Ann Dixon, *Secretary*
C. V. Buttelman, *Treasurer*
Fowler Smith, *Director*
William D. Revelli, *Director*
J. Leon Ruddick, *Director*

The Northwest Music Supervisors' Conference

On July 6, 1927, in Seattle, at the close of the business meeting of the music department of the National Education Association, there was organized The Northwest Music Supervisors' Conference, to include Washington, Oregon, Montana and Idaho.

CALENDAR OF MEETINGS

1929 Spokane, Washington
  Letha L. McClure,
    President
  Edna L. McKee, *Secretary*

1931 Spokane, Washington
  Frances Dickey, *President*
  Helen Coy Boucher,
    Secretary

1933 Seattle, Washington
  Anne Landsbury Beck,
    President
  Margaret Lee Maaske,
    Secretary

1935 Boise, Idaho
  Charles R. Cutts,
    President
  Berenice Barnard,
    Secretary

OFFICERS FOR 1935-1937

Ethel M. Henson, *President*
Donald Foltz, *First Vice-President*
Berenice Barnard, *Second Vice-President*
Andrew Loney, Jr., *Secretary*
W. C. Welke, *Treasurer*
R. F. Goranson, *Auditor*
Charles R. Cutts, *Director*
Marguerite V. Hood, *Director*

California Conference

At the annual meeting of the California Public School Music Conference held in San Francisco in March, 1929, it was unanimously voted to affiliate with the National as a new sectional conference.

The California Conference is the natural outcome of a gradual combining of city, county and sectional conference groups dating from about 1919.

The name was changed at the 1931 meeting to California Western School Music Conference.

CALENDAR OF MEETINGS

1931 Los Angeles, California
Herman Trutner, Jr.,
President
S. Grace Gantt, *Secretary*

1933 Oakland, California
Gertrude B. Parsons,
President
Edna O. Douthit,
Secretary

1935 Pasadena, California
Arthur G. Wahlberg,
President
Helen M. Garvin,
Secretary-Treasurer

OFFICERS FOR 1935-1937

Mary E. Ireland, *President*
S. Earle Blakeslee, *First Vice-President*
Alfred H. Smith, *Second Vice-President*
Silvia Garrison, *Secretary-Treasurer*
Amy Grau Miller, *Director*

The preceding account of the inception and growth of the music conference movement has been largely chronological, with only brief mention of important new features of successive meetings. Such a summary can give no idea of the supreme importance of these organizations in the development of school-music during the past fifteen years. Serving as a clearing house for ideas, drawing upon the entire country for oustanding leadership, demonstrating new types of excellence in all fields of school music

Presidents of the
Northwest Music Supervisors' Conference

LETHA L. McCLURE

FRANCES DICKEY NEWENHAM

ANNE LANDSBURY BECK

CHARLES R. CUTTS

ETHEL M. HENSON

Presidents of the California Western
School Music Conference

HERMAN TRUTNER, JR.

GERTRUDE B. PARSONS

ARTHUR G. WAHLBERG

MARY ELIZABETH IRELAND

education, burying differences and working for the common good, these conferences have, more than any other agency, brought about a development and expansion of music in the public schools which has no parallel in any other subject of the curriculum.

THE DALLAS MEETING OF THE DEPARTMENT OF SUPERINTENDENCE

It is fitting that the last event to be recorded in this history should be the great meeting at Dallas, Texas, of the Department of Superintendence. All meetings of this organization are educationally important, but the meeting held in Dallas the first week of March, 1927 was noteworthy because for the first time an entire general session was devoted to music and a special session was given over to a discussion of music education.

The general session alluded to took the form of a program consisting of three parts,—the singing of 800 boys and girls from the upper elementary grades under the direction of Sudie Williams, supervisor of music in the Dallas schools, an address by William F. Webster, superintendent of the Minneapolis schools, and the playing of the National High School Orchestra under the direction of Joseph E. Maddy. There were 270 players, gathered from thirty-eight states. They played with finesse and effectiveness a program from the works of Mendelssohn, Beethoven, Schumann, Handel, Tschaikowsky and Rimsky-

Korsakow. One hundred of these players had belonged to the National Orchestra which appeared in Detroit in 1926 at the first biennial meeting of the Music Supervisors' National Conference.

The discussion group consisted of leading superintendents, the members of the National Research Council for Music Education, and supervisors and teachers of music. The discussion was in charge of Peter W. Dykema. The speakers were superintendents Jesse H. Newlon of Denver, Herbert S. Weet of Rochester, P. P. Claxton of Tulsa, Florence M. Hale, Assistant State Commissioner of Maine, Thomas E. Finegan of Harrisburg, and Russell J. Condon of Cincinnati, president of the Department of Superintendence, whose vision made possible the emphasis placed upon music at the Dallas meeting. The speakers who represented the National Conference were Peter W. Dykema and Will Earhart.

Out of the discussion came the following memorable set of resolutions which were adopted unanimously:—

"1. We favor the inclusion of music in the curriculum on an equality with other basic subjects. We believe that with the growing complexity of civilization more attention must be given to the arts and that music offers possibilities as yet but partially realized for developing an appreciation of the finer things of life. We, therefore, recommend that all administrative officers take steps towards a more equitable adjustment of music in the educational program, involving time allotment, number and standard of teachers, and equipment provided.

"2. We favor an immediate extension of music study to all rural schools, in the belief that no single development will so greatly increase the effectiveness of their work and so greatly lessen the extreme differences now existing between rural and urban education. We recommend as a guide the *Course of Study for Music in Rural Schools*, approved by the Music Supervisors' National Conference.

"3. We believe that an adequate program of high school music instruction should include credit, equivalent to that given other basic subjects, for properly supervised music study carried on both in and out of school; moreover, the recognition of music by the high schools as a subject bearing credit toward graduation should carry with it similar recognition of its value by colleges and other institutions of higher education. We recommend further that the Department of Superintendence favor a study of present practices as to music credits.

"4. Recognizing the great interest manifested at this meeting toward making music a more vital element in education, we recommend that this subject shall continue to receive the attention of the Department of Superintendence, and be included in the discussion groups of its annual programs."

The report of the Committee on Resolutions,

given at the last business session of the Dallas
meeting, contained the following significant paragraph:—

"We would record our full appreciation of the
fine musical programs and art exhibits in connection
with this convention. They are good evidence that
we are rightly coming to regard music, art, and other
similar subjects as fundamental in the education of
American children. We recommend that they be
given everywhere equal consideration and support
with other basic subjects."

When in 1838 the Boston School Board authorized the introduction of music by public authority
as a regular subject of instruction, termed by the
trustees of the Boston Academy of Music the "Magna
Charta of Music Education in America," their action
was virtually a vote of confidence in the musical
possibilities inherent in children, brought about
largely through the activities of one man, Lowell
Mason. The action by the Department of Superintendence was equally a vote of confidence in the
work of the thousands of grade teachers and supervisors who have labored to make music a living
reality in the lives of children in the ninety years
which have intervened. The vote at Dallas was at
once a promise of co-operation and a challenge to
the school-music profession to bring to complete
fulfillment the great work remaining to be done in
music education.

CHAPTER IX

RECENT TRENDS AND DEVELOPMENTS IN MUSIC EDUCATION

The last decade of school music education coincides with that of the biennial plan of the National Conference and its six allied Conferences. This coincidence is not merely chronological. Every significant advance in every section of the country has been exhibited in the program activities of the conferences, not only by groups of children and youth in choral and orchestral demonstration, but by speakers who have discussed their educational significance. Many of these speakers have been superintendents and principals of schools. Their remarks have not only emphasized full acceptance of music as a school curriculum activity, but have expressed their expectation that music teachers will work in close co-operation with the regular teachers, the significance of which lies in the administrative conviction of the importance of music in well rounded child development. This official opinion is reinforced by the increasing desire of parents in every section that their children gain the power and skill to participate in group activities, especially in the contests and festivals, city, county, district, state and national, which every year are more and more focusing the attention of the public upon school music education.

The growth of the contest and festival movement has been very rapid. Its development has been traced by Joseph E. Maddy in his reports of 1928 and 1930 as conference chairman of instrumental affairs, from which we quote:—

"This report (1928) marks the conclusion of six years of activity on the part of the Committee on Instrumental Affairs, in which time the subject of instrumental music has grown from an experiment to a regular subject in many of the school systems in America. The success of the Committee is due in a large measure to the whole-hearted support and co-operation of the National Bureau for the Advancement of Music, through the untiring efforts of Mr. C. M. Tremaine, director of the Bureau and secretary of the Committee. The band contest development began in 1924. Prior to that time there was but one representative state contest, together with two or three others, each with three or four bands participating, and a so-called national contest, all these with a total entry list of probably less than sixty bands. In 1926 the Committee conducted or co-operated in the conduct of fifteen state, one interstate, and the first national contest on a basis of state units. The latter contest was held in Fostoria, Ohio, with thirteen bands in attendance, representing the winning bands from ten states. In 1927 the number of state contests increased to twenty, and the national contest, held at Council Bluffs, Iowa, brought twenty-three bands from fourteen states. A total of over 300 bands competed in the various state contests, culminating in the 1927 national band contest. . . . The National School Band Association was formed during the 1926 national band contest by the directors and members of the competing bands. The membership has grown to over 4000, and is expected to reach 15,000 in another year."

From Mr. Maddy's 1930 report:— "The number of state school band contests organized by the Committee or held with its co-operation increased from 30 in 1928 to 38 in 1929 and will probably be 43 or possibly more this year (1930). This means that the work has now been established in nearly all the states of the Union. . . . When it is realized that in 1923, when the Committee undertook to sponsor and stimulate these contests, there were but two or three states holding competitions of this kind, usually with few participants, the growth of this work . . . stands out in clearer relief.

"The Committee did not begin its co-operation with the school orchestra contests till 1928, four years after the activity had started with the bands, but here the growth has been relatively still greater, being helped materially by the interest aroused in the school band contest. During the very first year of its work in the orchestral field, the Committee assisted in 15 state contests and during the second (1929) in 30. It also held the first National High School Orchestra Contest last May, in Iowa City, Iowa, under the auspices of the University of Iowa. This year (1930) there will be at least six or eight additional states organized. . . .

"At the band contest last spring the name of the National School Band Association was changed to National School Band and Orchestra Association, and the division into two sections made, with a vice-president in charge of each."

Owing to the steadily increasing number of contests and festivals, involving more and more work in the selection of contest numbers for the various classifications, and in formulating rules and standards governing the contests, it became necessary in 1932 to form an orchestral association separate from the band association under the title National School Orchestra Association as it was originally organized. Since its organization in 1926 A. R. McAllister has been president of the National School Band Association and Adam P. Lesinsky has been president of the National School Orchestra Association since its organization in 1932. Both associations have worked in closest co-operation with the Committee on Instrumental Affairs of the National Conference under whose control the National Contests are held.

Early in the contest movement educators felt

that the intensely competitive factor lessened the educational value of the events. From this feeling grew the Competition-Festival, which gradually tended to supplant the original contest plan, and which by a new rating system allowed more than one group to have the same rating. By massing the rival groups into one large performing group, united in feeling and purpose, the main conditions incident to the true festival are secured.

The contest movement started in the Middle West, as did also the rating plan and the competition-festival movement, largely through the influence of Frank A. Beach, whose long and successful management of the state contests in Kansas brought him national recognition, in his appointment as chairman of the National Committee on Contests and Festivals.

A remarkable piece of co-operative effort and planning was the organization in 1925 of the New England Music Festival Association, largely through the initiative of Clifford V. Buttelman, who secured for the enterprise the active interest of the Rotary and Kiwanis clubs of Boston and also the Civic Music Association and the Advertising Club of that city. The New England Association has sponsored annual festivals in Boston since 1925. The New England High School Festival Orchestra, the New England High School Festival Chorus, and the New England School Band and Orchestra Contests continue as an-

nual features. In 1936 the New England High
School Band will be organized for the first time.
State contests were first organized in 1928. Prom-
inently identified with this movement are such leaders
as Mrs. William Arms Fisher, Harry E. Whittemore,
James D. Price, Francis Findlay and Walter Butterfield.

The rapid and spectacular development of instrumental music, with its growth in technical skill,
stimulated a similar effort on the part of vocal directors.   From the splendid singing of the three
National High School Choruses, under Hollis Dann
at Chicago in 1928 and 1930 and in Detroit in 1931
there came a realization of the infinite possibilities of
adolescent choral performance, resulting in new
standards of achievement in all forms of choral work.
This new interest in perfecting choral technique has
extended to training the adolescent voice in High
School classes. The striking success of class lessons
in vocal technique is marking a new era in music
education.

The problem of making music function in after-
school life in the home and community, which for
many years has perplexed music educators, recently
drew attention to the educational and leisure time
value of small instrumental and vocal ensembles as a
promising solution. The wealth of material ready
to hand for such activities, together with the ease of
forming such groups and their meeting in the or-

NATIONAL HIGH SCHOOL ORCHESTRA
AND (INSET) JOSEPH E. MADDY

CLIFFORD V. BUTTELMAN

JOSEPH E. MADDY

A. R. McALLISTER

ADAM P. LESINSKY

rinary home, has stimulated a movement in the direction of small group instruction which is extending rapidly through the high schools of the country. This movement and the wide discussion attending it, has called renewed attention to the purpose of public school music as avocational rather than vocational, and functioning in amateur rather than professional activities.

In an attempt to solve at least partially the problems presented by the varying musical capacities of children, a movement is gaining headway to form primary and intermediate school choirs, thus giving the more musical pupils opportunities for a richer musical development than is possible in the ordinary daily lesson which includes all the children. Working toward somewhat the same end, several school systems have experimented with creative music, so-called, and with results which seem to justify its becoming one of the teaching activities in all schools.

The radio is rapidly becoming a most effective factor in music education. Not only the fine concerts broadcast outside of school hours, including the Music Education Broadcasts sponsored by the Music Educators National Conference, but also the concerts given in school hours, notably by Walter Damrosch, the weekly instruction given by Charles A. Fullerton a few years ago to the rural school teachers of Iowa, and more recently the lessons in vocal and instrumental music by Mr. Maddy from the Ann Arbor studio and similar instruction given to the Cleveland schools by the music department of that city, all indicate that the present generation is witnessing what may grow into a revolutionary force in education.

The decade has brought forth a large amount of professional writing. The year books of the National Conference and the corresponding volumes of the Music Teachers National Association are full of inspiration for the modern music teacher. While their literary contents consist solely of papers prepared for professional meetings, these writings are of permanent worth; their style is cogent and readable, and the future historian will find them indispensable for a clear understanding of music education during the period, and of its theory and practice.

Equally significant and valuable are the large number of books pertaining to various phases of music education which have appeared in recent years, such as the following:—

Preparation and Presentation of the Operetta, by Frank A. Beach; *Staging School Operettas*, by Kenneth Umfleet; *Twenty Lessons in Conducting*, and *Music in the Grade Schools*, both by Karl W. Gehrkens; *Psychology of School Music Teaching*, by James L. Mursell and Mabelle Glenn; *Principles of Music Education*, and *Human Values in Music Education*, both by James L. Mursell; *Music for Public*

School Administrators, by Peter W. Dykema; *Problems in Public School Music*, by Jacob Kwalwasser; *Music to the Listening Ear, The Eloquent Baton*, and *The Meaning and Teaching of Music*, all by Will Earhart; *A Professionalized Study of Public School Music*, by Clara Josephine McCauley; *Music Integration in the Junior High School*, by Lilla Belle Pitts; *Fundamentals of Musicianship*, by Melville Smith and Max T. Krone; and *Teaching School Music*, by Alma M. Norton.

The Music Educators Journal (formerly *the Music Supervisors' Journal*), *Educational Music Magazine* (formerly *The Educational Music Bulletin*), and *School Music* are published several times a year. The first of these magazines is the official organ of the Music Educators' National Conference and the affiliated conferences. Its columns are devoted about equally to Conference affairs and articles of interest to the school music profession.

The present chapter has sketched the main trends in music education during the last ten years. The most potent and far reaching influence in this development has been the National Conference. With the appointment in 1930 of Clifford V. Buttelman as executive secretary, the Conference took a long-needed step in its organization, which, while previously working with high efficiency, needed a permanent secretary. The executive secretary, since the creation of that office, has kept in constant contact

with the entire Conference machinery. He attends
the meetings of all the affiliated Conferences, which
are scheduled to make this possible, and when there
are no meetings he keeps in touch with their officers.
He is the contact official of the Conferences and his
office at 64 East Jackson Boulevard, Chicago is the
clearing house for all Conference business. He is
the managing editor of the *Music Educators Journal*,
the Conference Year Book, and all other Conference
publications, such as the reports of the Research
Council and those of other special committees. The
office of executive secretary has made possible a closer
affiliation with many other associations, including the
Music Teachers National Association, the National
Association of Schools of Music, The National Federation of Music Clubs, the National Recreation Association, the American Choral and Festival Alliance,
and the rapidly increasing number of In and About
clubs.

The affairs of the National and affiliated conferences, financial, executive, promotive and educational are in the hands of presidents, executive committees, boards of directors, the National Research
Council and thirty-eight standing committees, numbering at least two hundred and fifty persons, chosen
for their efficiency in a special field. These committee groups are doing collectively what each conference member would like to do individually. They
are studying all phases of public school music and

are taking note of those of enough importance to have a hearing in the programs of the Conferences. The school music profession is becoming unified through the working organization of the National Conference, with the effect of vitalizing the relationship of every music teacher to the profession as a whole and to his individual colleagues.

BIBLIOGRAPHY

ALICE MORSE EARLE: *The Sabbath in Puritan New England* (Scribner, 1896)

WILLIAM ARMS FISHER: *Notes on Music in Old Boston* (Oliver Ditson Company, 1918)

Connecticut Quarterly, 1895

Boston Musical Gazette, Feb. 6, 1839

DANIEL GREGORY MASON, editor: *Music in America,* Vol. IV of *The Art of Music* (The National Society of Music)

HENRY C. LAHEE: *Annals of Music in America* (Marshall Jones Company, 1922)

American History and Encyclopedia of Music, History o American Music

Dwight's Journal of Music, 1852-1882, 40 volumes

American Supplement of Grove's Dictionary of Music ana Musicians; articles on Public Schools, Tune Books Conventions, etc. (Macmillan Co.)

M. T. N. A. Proceedings, 1906-1935

M. T. N. A. Reports, 1876-1906 (Library of Congress)

Books of Proceedings, Music Supervisors' National Conference, 1910-1927

Music Supervisors' Journal, 1914-1935

Books of Proceedings, N. E. A., beginning with 1884

School Music, 1900-1927, 27 volumes

BIBLIOGRAPHY

EDWIN N. C. BARNES: *Who's Who in Music Education,* Music Education, Washington, D. C., 1925

The Musician, November, 1905, and Volume V, 1900

ELLWOOD P. CUBBERLEY: *Public Education in the United States* (Houghton, Mifflin & Co.)

WILL EARHART and OSBOURNE MCCONATHY: *Music in Secondary Schools,* U. S. Government Bulletin, No. 40

F. L. RITTER: *Music in America* (Scribner, 1884)

NATHANIEL GOULD: *History of Church Music in America*

W. S. B. MATHEWS: *A Hundred Years of Music in America*

LOUIS C. ELSON: *History of American Music* (Macmillan Co.)

WILLIAM MASON: *Memories of a Musical Life,* Century Magazine, July, 1900

WILL S. MONROE: *Cyclopedia of Education,* article, *Music*

EDWARD DICKINSON: *Music in the History of the Western Church* (Scribner)

GEORGE P. UPTON: *Musical Memories* (A. C. McClurg & Co.)

THOMAS RYAN: *Recollections of an Old Musician* (E. P. Dutton)

W. S. B. MATHEWS, editor *Music,* 1892-1901

School Music Journal, 1885-1888

FRANCES M. DICKEY: *The Early History of Public School Music in the United States*

FRANK A. BEACH: *Preparation and Presentation of the Operetta* (Oliver Ditson Company)

KENNETH UMFLEET: *Staging School Operettas*

KARL W. GEHRKENS: *Twenty Lessons in Conducting* (Oliver Ditson Company); and *Music in the Grade Schools*

JAMES L. MURSELL and MABELLE GLENN: *Psychology of School Music Teaching*

JAMES L. MURSELL: *Principles of Music Education;* and *Human Values in Music Education*

PETER W. DYKEMA: *Music for Public School Administrators*

JACOB KWALWASSER: *Problems in Public School Music*

WILL EARHART: *Music to the Listening Ear; The Eloquent Baton;* and *The Meaning and Teaching of Music*

CLARA JOSEPHINE MCCAULEY: *A Professionalized Study of Public School Music*

LILLA BELLE PITTS: *Music Integration in the Junior High School*

MELVILLE SMITH and MAX T. KRONE: *Fundamentals of Musicanship*

ALMA M. NORTON: *Teaching School Music*

GLENN H. WOODS: *School Orchestras and Bands* (Oliver Ditson Company)

RAYMOND N. CARR: *Building the School Orchestra*

J. E. MADDY and T. P. GIDDINGS: *Instrumental Technique for Orchestra and Band*

INDEX

INDEX

316

INDEX

INDEX

INDEX

319

INDEX

MADDY, J. E., 197, 198, 199, 201, 209, 263, 269, 271, 274, 276, 297, 302, 307

"Magna Charta" of Music Education, 55, 300

Manual of Instruction, Boston Academy of Music, 27, 28, 38

MARSHALL, LEONARD B., 134

MASON, ARTHUR W., 278

MASON, LOWELL, 14, 18, 25, 26, 27, 28, 29, 30, 31, 36, 37, 38, 39, 49, 55, 56, 57, 60, 74, 77, 79, 83, 90, 95, 102, 107, 111, 229, 263, 286, 300

MASON, LUTHER WHITING, 56, 66, 90, 100, 102, 103, 104, 105, 106, 121, 134, 135, 136, 138, 232, 234

MASON, WILLIAM, 32, 84, 87, 139

MATTHEWS, W. S. B., 32, 80, 83, 210

MCALLISTER, A. R., 294, 304

MCBRIDE, HELEN, 289, 291

MCCLURE, LETTA L., 295

MCCONATHY, OSBOURNE, 135, 170, 185, 242, 243, 254, 257, 264, 265, 267, 272, 278
  with Haake, 204

MCCORMACK, MARY, 280, 281

MCINERNEY, ANNA LOUISE, 288

MCKEE, EDNA L., 295

MCLAUGHLIN, JAMES, 136, 137, 282

Memory Contest, 175, 214, 228

MEYER, LENA, 293

MIESSNER, W. OTTO, 187, 204, 254, 264, 272, 278

MILAM, LENA, 293

MILLER, CHARLES H., 201, 249, 254, 264, 278

MILLER, MRS. CHARLES H., 266

MITCHELL, ALBERT G., 194

MONNIER, W. D., 167

MOORE, HENRY E., 26

MORE, GRACE VAN DYKE, 291

MORGAN, RUSSELL V., 197, 198, 264, 272, 279

Music, church, 4
  in colleges, 88
  in elementary grades, 174
  in high schools, 165, 250, 265
  public schools, 75, 86, 107, 114, 163, 219, 252
  see also "Literature of"
  readers, 175
    see also "Literature"

Music Discrimination Contest, 274

Music Educators Journal, 275

Music Educators National Conference, 274, 288, 292, 298
  Affiliations, 309, 310

Music Supervisors' Journal, 276, 277

Music Supervisors' National Conference, 171, 197, 209, 214, 219, 224, 245, 246, 250, 251, 253, 254, 256, 260, 261, 263, 264, 265, 266, 269, 273, 274, 275, 279, 283, 285, 301, 304

Music Teachers National Association, 87, 97, 122, 140, 168, 219, 222, 232, 242, 250, 310

Musical Convention, 29, 33

NATIONAL
  Association of Schools of Music, 310
  Band Contest, 200, 302
  Bureau for the Advancement of Music, 198, 208, 214, 227, 302, 303
  Community Music League, 227
  Conservatory, Committee on, 265
  Education Association, 90, 129, 168, 223, 230, 234, 237, 239, 241, 243, 245, 248, 256
  Federation of Music Clubs, 227, 310
  Federation of School Music Teachers, 237

320

INDEX

INDEX

INDEX